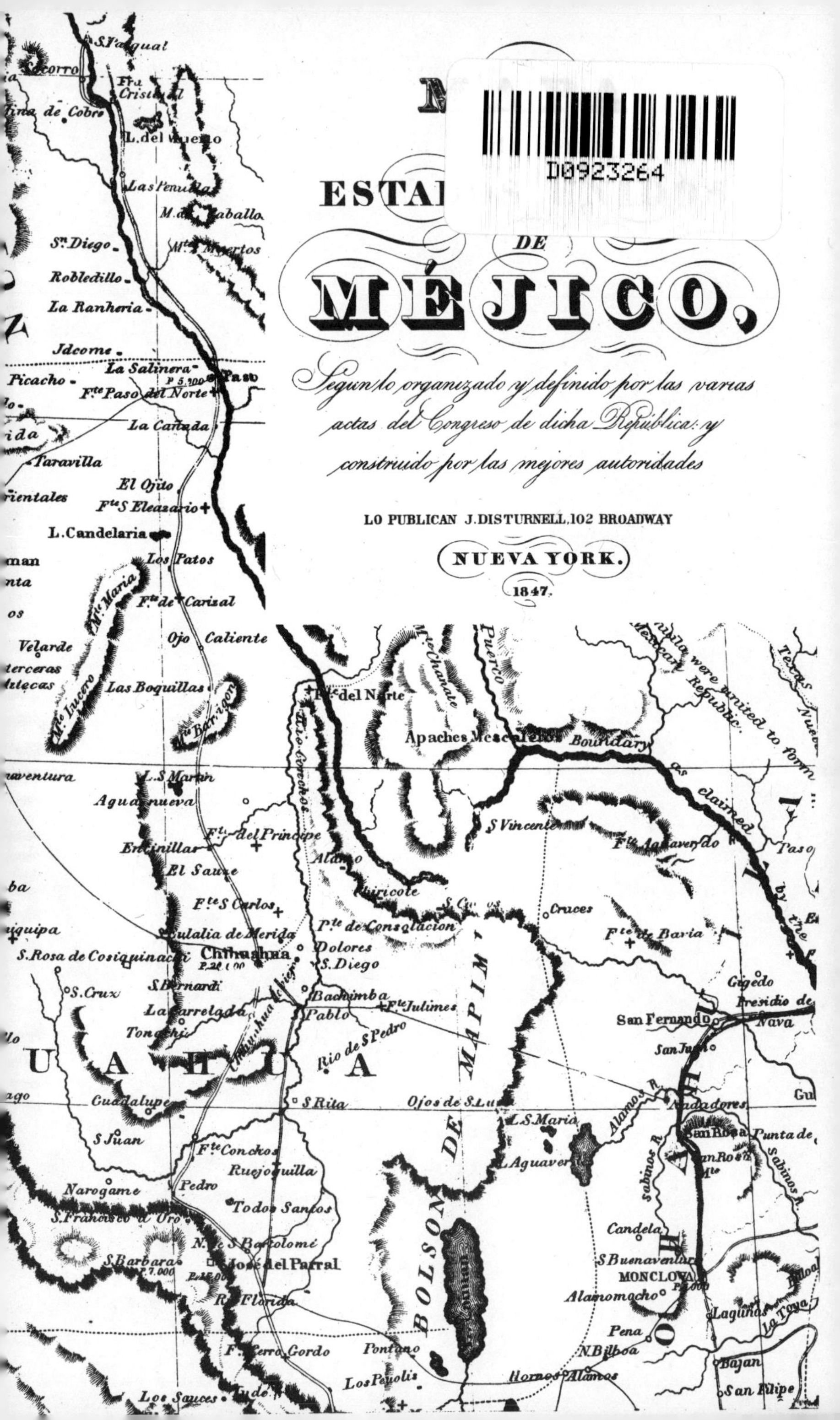

ESTA
DE
MÉJICO,
Segun lo organizado y definido por las varias actas del Congreso de dicha República: y construido por las mejores autoridades
LO PUBLICAN J. DISTURNELL, 102 BROADWAY
NUEVA YORK.
1847.
D0923264
Socorro
Fra Cristobal
Mina de Cobre
L. del Muerto
Las Penuelas
M. de Caballo
Sn Diego
Mts Muertos
Robledillo
La Ranheria
Jdcome
La Salinera
Picacho
Fte Paso del Norte
Paso
La Cañada
Taravilla
El Ojito
Fte S Eleazario
L. Candelaria
Los Patos
Mte Maria
Fte de Carizal
Ojo Caliente
Velarde
Las Boquillas
Mte Lucero
Mte Barrigon
L. S Martin
Aguanueva
Fte del Principe
Encinillas
El Sauce
Fte S Carlos
Eulalia de Merida
Chihuahua
S. Rosa de Cosiquinachi
S. Bernardi
S. Cruz
La Carrelada
Tonachi
Guadalupe
S Juan
Fte Conchos
Ruejoquilla
Narogame
Pedro
Todos Santos
S. Francisco d' Oro
N. S. Bartolomé
S. Barbara
José del Parral
Florida
Cerro Gordo
Los Sauces
Rio Conchos
Fte del Norte
Mte Chanate
Puerco
Apaches Mescaleros
Boundary as claimed by the
Mexican Republic
Texas
S Vincente
Fte Aguaverdo
Alamo
Chiricole
Pte de Consolacion
Dolores
S. Diego
Bachimba
Pablo
Fte Julimes
Rio de S Pedro
S Rita
Ojos de S. Lucas
Cruces
Fte de Baria
Gigedo
Presidio de
San Fernando
Nava
San Juan
Alamo R.
L. S. Maria
L. Aguaverde
San Rosa
Punta de
Sabinos R.
Candela
S Buenaventura
MONCLOVA
Alamomocho
Lagunas
La Toya
Pena
N. Bilboa
Bajan
San Filipe
Pontano
Los Peulis
Hornos
Alamos
BOLSON DE MAPIMI
U A H U A

Stuart Library
of Western Americana
UNIVERSITY OF
THE PACIFIC
STOCKTON,
CALIFORNIA

TOO FAR NORTH: TOO FAR SOUTH

GREAT WEST AND INDIAN SERIES XXXV

Too Far North...
Too Far South

by

Odie B. Faulk

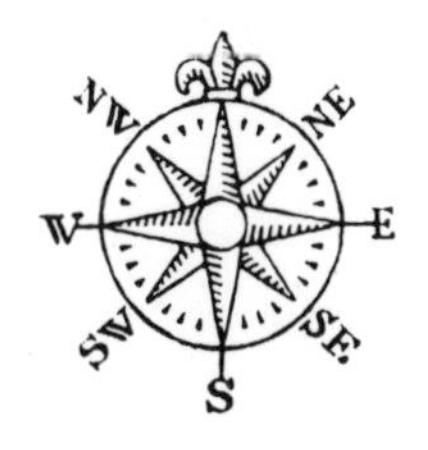

Westernlore Press...1967...Los Angeles 90041

LIBRARY
OCT 16 1968
UNIVERSITY OF THE PACIFIC
191145
Western Americana
Western Americana
F
786
F26

COPYRIGHT 1967
BY ODIE B. FAULK, PH.D.

Library of Congress Catalog Number 67-19671

PRINTED IN THE UNITED STATES OF AMERICA BY WESTERNLORE PRESS

Dedicated to

PROFESSOR SEYMOUR V. CONNOR

Scholar and Friend — to whom I owe many debts

INTRODUCTION

IN A STORY entitled "The Surveyors Were Sober," which appeared in the popular Phoenix newspaper Sunday Supplement, *Arizona Days and Ways,* on August 29, 1965, Roscoe Willson discussed two of the more popular misconceptions held about why the southern boundary of Arizona suddenly turns at the intersection of 31° 20′ north latitude and 111° west longitude and runs in a straight line to the Colorado River just below Yuma. According to these legends, the boundary takes a northwesterly turn either because the surveyors were drunk on tequila and thought they were continuing due west, or because they were hot and thirsty and decided to head for Yuma, the nearest place to get a beer. Of course neither of these reasons is correct, but they do illustrate the widespread ignorance about the true reasons for the peculiar boundary which was drawn to separate the United States from Mexico.

Even more widely believed — and equally untrue — is the story that the Gadsden Purchase was made to secure a transcontinental railroad route. This is the reason for the purchase cited in almost every work of history which touches upon the subject. The necessity for the acquisition stemmed from reasons much more complicated and involved, as this study attempts to show. The Treaty of Guadalupe Hidalgo, concluded in 1848 at the end of the Mexican War, gave the United States the majority of the present Southwest. But the boundary had to be surveyed. Not until seven years had passed, a new treaty had been negotiated, and three-quarters of a million dollars had been spent was the line finally marked. The events connected with this study did not take place altogether in the Southwest. Bureaucratic functionaries and political appointees in both Washington, D. C., and in Mexico City were involved; the futures of both Antonio López de Santa Anna of Mexico and the Democratic and Whigs parties in the United States were changed during the course of the dispute. Political chicanery was intertwined with national interests, while personal gain went hand-in-hand with patriotic pronouncement. No matter where the boundary was set in any of the agreements or treaties, neither side was satisfied. For some the boundary was too far north; for others it was too far south. It is difficult in this confused morass to distinguish the heroes from the villains; on both sides the greatest blunders were made from the purest of motives, while gains resulted from incompetence in high places.

In preparing this study I have incurred several debts which I here acknowledge. Professor Seymour V. Connor, of Texas Technological College in Lubbock, first proposed this study to me in the fall of 1959, and since that time he has guided and encouraged me in numerous ways. Professor John Alexander Carroll of The University of Arizona at Tucson stimulated me to continue working on the boundary story by publishing a portion of it in *Arizona and the West,* a journal he founded and edited for five years. The staff of the Southwest Collection at Texas Technological College aided me by securing several imprints and by digging endlessly through their holdings. Mr. Frank Hillary, of Tucson, aided in the work with Mexican imprints by lending of his knowledge and time. My thanks are also extended to Mr. W. J. Holliday, collector of Western Americana, for the materials he brought together and deposited at the Arizona Pioneers' Historical Society at Tucson; many of the rarest documents cited in this work are from the Holliday Collection. Mr. Robert B. McCoy, President of Rio Grande Press, further encouraged the completion of this study by his interest in the subject. Finally, I acknowledge the debt I owe Mr. Bert M. Fireman, Executive Vice President of the Arizona Historical Foundation of Phoenix, for pointing out several facts which I had overlooked; his extended conversations with me on this subject were of great aid.

ODIE B. FAULK
Research Historian,
Arizona Pioneers' Historical Society.

CONTENTS

ILLUSTRATIONS

MAPS

TOO FAR NORTH: TOO FAR SOUTH

I

PROLOGUE

ON THE AFTERNOON of May 25, 1848, a carriage approached the village of Querétaro, then the temporary capital of the Mexican republic. Inside the carriage were Nathan Clifford, the Attorney General of the United States, and Ambrose H. Sevier, American Senator from Ohio and chairman of the Senate Foreign Relations Committee. Despite the fact that they were accredited American commissioners on their way to exchange ratifications of a peace treaty, the two men doubtless were nervous; until very recently a state of war had existed between the two republics, and the flag of the United States was still flying above the *Palacio Nacional* in Mexico City.

About ten miles from Querétaro the carriage was met by Luis de la Rosa, the Mexican Secretary of State and Relations, along with a number of govermental functionaries. After the introductions were completed, Secretary Rosa joined Sevier and Clifford in the carriage, and they proceeded toward the city. They passed through the gates of Querétaro at five o'clock that afternoon and were greeted by a scene of noise and confusion. Fireworks were exploding, and bands marched in every direction, each playing a different tune. The citizens of the city were celebrating the acceptance of the Treaty of Guadalupe Hidalgo by the Mexican Congress.[1] The House of Deputies had passed it by a vote of fifty-one to thirty-five on May 19, and the Senate that afternoon of May 25 had accepted it by a vote of thirty-three to four. However, not all the population seemed pleased; despite the presence of Señor Rosa, the American commissioners' carriage was stoned as it passed through the city streets by unhappy Mexicans shouting *"Viva la Guerra! Abajo la Paz!"* (Hurrah for War! Down with Peace!)

At noon the following day, May 26, Secretary Rosa introduced Clifford to the President of the Mexican Republic, Manuel de la Peña y Peña. Sevier was absent because of illness. The American delegate presented his credentials, then made a short address to the president and to the cabinet members and other civil and military officials of the government who had gathered:

> We have come . . . for the exchange of ratifications of the treaty signed at Guadalupe Hidalgo, with the amendments made to it by the Senate at Washington. This treaty, so amended, having been approved by the Congress of Mexico, an exchange of ratifications is all that now remains for the complete re-establishment of peace between the two countries . . . . Sister republics, may the two countries ever maintain the most friendly relations in all their intercourse.

[1] "Treaty of Peace, Friendship, Limits and Settlement between the United States of America and the Mexican Republic, concluded at Guadalupe Hidalgo, on the 2d Day of February, in the year 1848," in William M. Malloy (comp.), *Treaties, Conventions, International Acts, Protocols and Agreements Between the United States of America and Other Powers, 1776-1909* (2 vols., Washington, 1910), I, 1109-1113; see also George P. Hammond (ed.), *The Treaty of Guadalupe Hidalgo* (Berkeley: The Friends of the Bancroft Library, 1949) for an excellent study of this treaty. For an understanding of the role of Nicolas P. Trist in the negotiation of the treaty, see Louis M. Sears, "Nicolas P. Trist, Diplomat With Ideals," *Mississippi Valley Historical Review,* XI (June 1924), 85-98.

President Peña responded in the same formal manner: "As the head of this republic, I desire nothing more ardently than that our treaty may be the immutable base of that constant harmony and good understanding which should prevail with sincerity between the two republics, for the advancement of their happiness. . . ."[2]

Five days were consumed in conference, with some delay caused by the slowness in preparing a Mexican copy of the agreements necessary to put the peace treaty into effect. Finally the exchange of ratifications of the treaty took place on May 30. At that time Secretary Rosa asked that the American army of occupation remain in Mexico City until the Mexican authorities could take the necessary precautions to avoid disorders during the transfer of authority. Such arrangements were soon completed, and at six o'clock on the morning of June 12 the Stars and Stripes were replaced above the National Palace with the Eagle and Serpent. The customary honors were paid to both standards during the ceremony. The large crowd of Mexicans who had gathered in the *Zocalo* to watch the ceremony remained perfectly quiet throughout the proceedings, and that same day the American troops began withdrawing to Vera Cruz for embarkation.[3] The fighting was over.

A special messenger arrived in Washington, D. C., on the morning of July 4, 1848, with the signed copy of the Treaty of Guadalupe Hidalgo. President Polk immediately instructed the

[2]Clifford and Sevier to James Buchanan (Secretary of State), Querétaro, May 25 and May 30, 1848; "Address of the Commissioners of the United States to the President of the Mexican Republic, on delivering their credentials;" and "Reply of the President," in *House Executive Document* 50, 30 Cong., 2 Sess., 74-76.

[3]George L. Rives, *The United States and Mexico, 1821-1848* (2 vols., New York, 1913), II, 651-653; Horatio M. Ladd, *History of the War with Mexico* (New York, 1883), 312.

Secretary of State to prepare the necessary papers so that the treaty could be proclaimed on the American anniversary of independence. This formal proclamation by the president officially ended the Mexican War and established peace, settling all differences between the two republics — or so everyone thought. Yet within five years the two nations again would be at the brink of war because of points of contention unwittingly written into that same "Treaty of Peace, Friendship, Limits and Settlement."

II

ORGANIZING THE JOINT BOUNDARY COMMISSION

ARTICLE V of the Treaty of Guadalupe Hidalgo delineated a new boundary between the United States and Mexico, and provided that a joint commission, comprising officials of each nation, should be appointed to run and mark the international line; the record of their acts would then become a part of the treaty and "have the same force as if it were inserted therein." On August 12, 1848, the American Congress appropriated $50,000 for the expenses that would be involved in the survey, and for the salaries of the officers of the commission.[1]

In searching for a boundary commissioner, President Polk decided upon Major William Hemsley Emory, an officer of the Corps of Topographical Engineers. Emory had been born in Queen Anne's County, Maryland on September 7, 1811, the son and grandson of patriots who had fought in the Revolutionary War and the War of 1812 respectively. He entered the United States Military Academy at the age of fifteen, and graduated

[1]Buchanan to John B. Weller, Washington, January 24, 1849, *Senate Executive Document* 34, 31 Cong., 1 Sess., Part I, 2-3. Hereafter cited as *SED* 34.

with the Class of 1831. Accepting a commission as brevet second lieutenant in the army, he was assigned to the Fourth Artillery. During the next five years he saw duty at Forts McHenry and Severn in Maryland; he was at Charleston Harbor, South Carolina, during the Nullification Controversy; other assignments included duty at Forts Hamilton and Lafayette, New York, and in the war on the Creek Indians during 1836. Emory resigned his commission on September 30, 1836, at the invitation of the Secretary of War to accept an appointment as an assistant United States civil engineer; this was done in order that he might be eligible for an appointment to the Corps of Topographical Engineers, then in the process of creation.[2] The Topographical Engineers was established as a separate entity in 1838, and on July 7 that year Emory was commissioned a first lieutenant in the organization.

During the next eight years he was employed in various tasks. From 1839 to 1842 he worked on harbor improvements along the Delaware River; from 1842 to 1844 he served as an assistant in the Topographical Bureau at the nation's capital; and from 1844 to 1846 he was a principal assistant on the Northeastern boundary survey between the United States and Canada. In the latter capacity he received the high commendation of the British Commissioner for his work in continuing the survey during the winter months along the mountains separating the drainages of the St. Lawrence and the Atlantic seaboard. Such employments

[2]A part of the Corps of Engineers from 1813 to 1838, the Corps of Topographical Engineers was created a separate branch of the army in the latter year. For a quarter of a century thereafter the Corps was active in many civil engineering works of the federal government, but it gained its real prominence in exploring the newly acquired American West. In 1863 the Corps was again consolidated with the Engineers. During its existence it attracted the highest standing graduates of West Point to its ranks, and many of the most prominent officers of the pre-Civil War era served in it.

were a mere apprenticeship, however, for the busy decade ahead for him.

With the outbreak of the Mexican War in 1846, Emory was assigned to the Army of the West, then being organized in Missouri by Brigadier General Stephen Watts Kearny. His title was chief engineer, but in addition he served as acting assistant adjutant general for the command. His task as chief engineer was to produce a report giving "some idea of the regions traversed," yet at the same time he was to "perform any military duty which shall be assigned to you . . . ." Kearny took Santa Fe and New Mexico without firing a shot, then divided his command into three parts. Some of the men were to stay at Santa Fe; another group was to march southward under Colonel Alexander W. Doniphan; and the third part was to go to California under the personal command of Kearny. Emory went with the latter group, and at San Pascual on December 6, 1846, he was placed in command of a squad of dragoons during that famous battle.[3] For his bravery in the engagement he was breveted a captain. The following month, as the Army of the West overcame all remaining resistance in California, he participated in the skirmishes at San Gabriel and the Plains of the Mesa, for which he was breveted a major.

Out of his experiences with the Army of the West came his *Notes of a Military Reconnoissance from Fort Leavenworth, in Missouri, to San Diego, in California,* printed in 1848 by order of Congress in an edition of ten thousand copies. The book immediately popularized the new Southwest, for it contained far more than just "some idea" of the area traversed. Accompanying it were the finest maps ever made to that time of the region,

[3]For an excellent study of this controversial engagement, see Arthur Woodward, *Lances at San Pascual* (San Francisco: California Historical Society, 1948).

comments about the flora and fauna, and estimates of the mineral wealth.[4] Following the conquest of California, Emory was transferred to a regiment from Maryland and the District of Columbia, with which he served as a lieutenant colonel of volunteers at Vera Cruz and Mexico City. When peace was restored, he returned to Washington; thus he was available for a new assignment when Polk began looking for a boundary commissioner. However, the president, in offering the office to Emory, insisted that the soldier resign his commission. Emory declined the post because of Polk's stipulation; therefore he was attached to the Commission as chief astronomer and commander of the military escort.

President Polk next offered the post of boundary commissioner to ex-Senator Ambrose H. Sevier, who had been defeated for re-election in November of 1848. However, Sevier died on December 31, 1848, before the Senate could act on his nomination. Polk on January 16, 1849, offered the post of Commissioner to John B. Weller of Ohio, who accepted the task and who subsequently was confirmed by the Senate. Weller had been born on February 22, 1812, in Montgomery, Ohio. He graduated from the public schools of his native state and studied at Miami University, then read law in the office of Jesse Corwin. In 1832 he was admitted to the Ohio bar, and for several years he was the prosecuting attorney of Butler County. In 1838, as a Democrat, he presented himself as a candidate for Congress and was elected; the same success attended his campaign of 1840 and 1842. When the Mexican War began, he enlisted as a private in an Ohio regiment, and by his own merit and daring rose

[4]Emory, *Notes of a Military Reconnoissance . . ., House Executive Document* 41, 30 Cong., 1 Sess.; reprinted as Ross Calvin (ed.), *Lieutenant Emory Reports* (Albuquerque: University of New Mexico Press, 1951).

John B. Weller

— Courtesy California State Library.

to the rank of colonel. At the end of the war he resigned his commission and returned to Ohio, where he made an unsuccessful bid for the office of governor. Polk took care of the defeated Democrat by appointing him United States Boundary Commissioner.

The Whigs, who would take office on March 4, 1849, following their victory the previous November, were very bitter at Polk's appointment of a Commissioner. They felt that the act constituted a sort of "midnight appointment," and that they had been cheated out of one of the spoils of office. Moreover, they contended that Weller's appointment was illegal. A bill to this effect was introduced in the House on February 28, 1849; the reasoning behind it was that the Congressional appropriation of $50,000 for running and marking the boundary, made the previous August, had contained no provision for the salaries of the Commissioner. Another amendment to the same act provided that no salary could be paid to the Commissioner "when the appointment of such commissioner . . . was made without authority of law."[5] Despite the fact that both these provisions failed to pass the Senate, they did indicate the strong partisan feelings in Congress, and they foreshadowed the subsequent attempts to discredit Weller.

The office of United States Surveyor went not to a politico, but to an eminently qualified civil engineer, Andrew Belcher Gray. Born in Norfolk, Virginia, on July 6, 1820, he was educated for his profession in a unique way — at an early age he was apprenticed to Andrew Talcott, an astronomer and former military engineer of great repute. While still a teenager, Gray worked with Talcott on the survey of the Mississippi Delta. Then, like many another adventurous Southern lad, he decided his destiny

[5]*Congressional Globe,* 30 Cong., 2 Sess., 617.

coincided with that of the new Republic of Texas. In 1839 he enlisted in the Texas Navy; the following year he served as surveyor for Texas on the joint commission delineating the boundary between the Lone Star Republic and the United States. Following this experience he went north for the exploration and survey of the Keweenaw Peninsula of Michigan, as an employee of the War Department of the United States. Afterwards he returned to Texas and fought the Indians as a member of the already famous Texas Rangers. Such was his background in December of 1848 when Polk nominated him as Surveyor.

The fifth article of the Treaty of Guadalupe Hidalgo, in addition to establishing the boundary between the United States and Mexico, provided that the boundary commissions of the two nations should meet in San Diego, California, by May 30, 1849. Since these officials for the United States were not confirmed until January of that year, it became imperative for the Commissioner to organize his party quickly and get it on its way. The survey had been placed under the orders of the Department of State, and on January 24 Secretary James Buchanan wrote Weller, "No time should be lost in organizing the commission on our part, preparatory to its departure for the place of destination."[6]

Before Weller left for San Diego, he received full orders concerning his duties. He was directed to collect information on quicksilver, precious metals, ores, and other substances in the vicinity of the boundary during the course of the survey; he was to keep full records and make a map of the country traversed; he was to secure scientific data concerning the flora and fauna of the region; and he was to make recommendations concerning the building of a road, canal, or railway on or within one marine

[6]Buchanan to Weller, Washington, January 24, 1849, *SED* 34, Part I, 2-3.

Andrew B. Gray

—*From* The A. B. Gray Report.
Courtesy Mr. W. Edwin Gledhill.

league (approximately 3.5 miles) of the Gila River, as provided for in Article VI of the Treaty of Guadalupe Hidalgo.[7]

As Weller was a politician and not a scientist or engineer, he, of course, could not be expected to do all these things personally. The surveying and making of the maps would be the responsibility of Gray and Emory. The scientific information was to be included in the report Emory would make as a Topographical Engineer, and for the purpose of collecting this data Emory procured the services of Dr. Charles Christopher Parry. Born in England in 1825, Parry at the age of nine had moved to the United States, where his family settled in the state of New York. He graduated from Union College in 1842, then earned his M.D. from Columbia in 1846. At Columbia he came under the influence of the prominent botanist John Torrey, and gradually his interests, as well as a major portion of his work, were centered on botany and geology. In fact, prior to his appointment to the Boundary Commission in 1849, he had worked on the geological surveys of Wisconsin, Iowa, and Minnesota. With the Commission he was listed as an "assistant surveyor and computer." In actuality, it was his task to collect the specimens of plants and animals and to make notes concerning the geology of the region.

To assist Emory in the astronomical work of the survey, the Corps of Topographical Engineers sent along Captain Edmund La Follette Hardcastle and Lieutenant Amiel Weeks Whipple. The captain had been born in Maryland, and had graduated from West Point in 1846, standing fifth in his class. Entering the Corps of Topographical Engineers that same year, he was breveted a first lieutenant and then a captain during the Mexican War for his bravery, especially at Molino del Rey. Whipple

[7]Buchanan to Weller, Washington, February 13, 1849, *idid.*, 3-6.

was a native of Massachusetts, and likewise was a graduate of West Point, class of 1841. During the Mexican War he had traversed the Southwest, and thus was more familiar with conditions in the vicinity of the boundary than any other member of the Commission except Emory.

Weller soon organized his party, which consisted in all of thirty-nine men; in addition there was the army escort, which would join the Commission at San Diego. The Commissioner was at his home in Ohio when he set out for the rendezvous with the Mexican commission; he chose to journey down the Mississippi River, and sailed from there on March 2 for Panama. Emory, Gray, and their assistants were in the East, and made separate arrangements. Major Emory had the responsibility of getting the necessary scientific instruments to San Diego. The heavier of these he shipped on the steamer *Panama,* a United States Pacific mail steamer bound for California by way of the Straits of Magellan, under the care of Captain Hardcastle. Then he embarked on another ship, this one going from New York to Panama; he reached the western side of the Isthmus on March 17, just one day behind Commissioner Weller. Gray left New York on February 22 and reached Panama on April 1. All three men, as well as their various assistants and servants, found travel very difficult, however, for they were caught up in the gold rush then underway. More than four thousand men were congregated at Panama City trying to get transportation to California.

President Polk's confirmation of the discovery of gold in California in December of 1848 had touched off a mass exodus for the digs. Every available boat along the east coast, including many that were not seaworthy, was pressed into service. Most of those seeking to get to the new Eldorado in those first months preferred to make the journey by sea. The usual route was by boat to the mouth of the Chagres River in Panama, a trip that previously had required only eight to twelve days, but in early 1849 took approximately one month. The depth of the bar at Chagres was only thirteen feet; therefore ocean-going vessels had to anchor off the coast and discharge their passengers into small native boats. Travelers then made their way to the head of the Chagres in those conveyances, from which point they could walk or hire mules for an overland trek of twenty miles to Panama City on the west coast. Once there, the traveler had to secure passage on a steamer bound for California — not an easy task, for men were willing to fight, even die, for a berth. Thus the entire commission found itself stranded at that port city for more than a month.

Emory quickly reconciled himself to the delay and whiled away the time by unpacking his instruments — those that he had with him — and setting up an observatory. Thus he made good use of the delay to instruct his assistants, and to make observations for latitude and longitude, magnetic dip and intensity, and other phenomena, which he carefully recorded. These findings later were published in the fifth volume of the proceedings of the American Academy of Arts and Sciences, findings that were made despite the fact that Emory and his men were in Panama during the rainy season, and cholera and yellow fever were raging through the land.

The first available ship bound for California proved to be the *Panama,* which had rounded the Horn and steamed northward while the members of the commission waited. Weller was able to obtain only ten berths aboard the ship — through the influence of William Nelson, the American Consul. He chose to include Gray and Emory, along with two of his personal servants, in those to be taken, leaving Whipple, Parry, and the vast majority of his party behind when he sailed on May 17. The first of many bitter quarrels broke out at this point, especially over who would pay for the rations of the men remaining behind.[8] Whipple managed to secure passage for Parry and himself on the *Oregon,* which sailed for California on May 23. The remainder of the commission found transportation at a later date.

Weller, Gray, and Emory arrived at San Diego on June 1, 1849, only one day late for the meeting set in the Treaty of Guadalupe Hidalgo. Emory noted that the town had changed but little since his previous acquaintance with it in 1846-1847. In fact, he wrote that the news of the discovery of gold in northern California had produced "less commotion in that quiet town than in New York or Panama. Fortunately for us, it did not feel the effect until the reaction came from the Atlantic side, some months after our arrival."[9] Had gold fever infected the town at that time, no laborers could have been secured and no detail of soldiers for escort duty would have been available. On June 16, Weller wrote of the disturbances in the town caused by the gold rush, stating that "it may be found wholly impracticable to prosecute the work [of surveying] from this direction beyond [the Colorado River]." He also noted that his expenses had been far greater than anticipated. "I fear," he wrote, "the appropriation made by the act of Congress on August 12, 1848, will be quite exhausted soon after the work is commenced . . . . The Congress of 1848, I am sure, could not have anticipated the state of affairs in this country, else the appropriation would have

[8]See various letters, *ibid.,* 39-44.

[9]Emory, *Report of the United States and Mexican Boundary Commission, Senate Executive Document* 108, 34 Cong., 1 Sess. (2 vols.), I, 3; reprinted in 1967 by the Rio Grande Press. Hereafter cited as Emory, *Report.*

been much more liberal."[10] Congress would later have this fact brought forcefully home to it, for the total cost of running and marking the Mexican boundary would exceed the original appropriation some fifteen times.

Major Emory, who had the additional duty of commanding the military escort of the Boundary Commission, found two detachments of troops waiting for him at San Diego. Company A of the 1st Dragoons, consisting of sixty-one men, was headed by Lieutenant Cave J. Couts; and Company H of the 2nd Infantry, consisting of twenty-two men, was headed by Captain Julius Hayden. Couts was a native of Tennessee. Appointed to the Military Academy by Congressman James K. Polk in 1838, Couts graduated thirty-seventh in a class of thirty-nine in 1843. He saw duty in Louisiana and the Indian Territory prior to the Mexican War; although promoted to first lieutenant in February of 1847, he did not get a transfer to the scene of action until after the battles had all been won and the fighting was over. In June of 1848 he was ordered to accompany a battalion marching from Monterrey, Mexico, to garrison duty in California,[11] and was serving there when the Boundary Commission arrived. Captain Hayden, a New Yorker by birth, was not a West Pointer. He had entered the army in 1839 as a second lieutenant of the 2nd Infantry, had fought at Contreras and Churubusco during the Mexican War, and had been breveted for bravery during the conflict. After the war the 2nd Infantry had been transferred to California, and Hayden went with it.

[10]Weller to John M. Clayton (Secretary of State), San Diego, June 16, 1849, *SED* 34, Part I, 27.

[11]For the story of this trek, see Henry F. Dobyns (ed.), *Hepah, California! The Journal of Cave Johnson Couts* (Tucson: Arizona Pioneers' Historical Society, 1961).

Although the American Boundary Commission arrived at San Diego one day late for the appointed rendezvous, it had to wait for more than a month for the Mexican counterpart to arrive. Shortly after reaching San Diego, Commissioner Weller received a letter from the American Consul at San Blas, Mexico, stating that the Mexican Commission had sailed on June 24 from that port on a British vessel. On July 3 the Mexican Commission arrived at San Diego, accompanied by approximately 150 troops. The Commissioner for that republic proved to be a politician, true enough, but a politician who was a soldier and engineer by profession — General Pedro García Conde.

General Conde was born in Arizpe, Sonora, on February 8, 1806. He joined the Spanish army at the presidio of San Carlos de Cerro Gordo as a cadet in 1818, and served at various frontier posts. The successful termination of the Mexican Revolution in 1821 found him on the winning side, and by 1828 he was a captain of engineers. Five years later he was in Chihuahua, where he completed the first geographical map of that state.[12] In 1837 he was made subdirector of the Military College in Mexico City, and while there he directed the reconstruction of the National Palace. He was promoted to brigadier general in 1843, and the following year he was serving as Secretary of War and Marine in the national government. The end of the Mexican War saw him elected to the national senate, from which post he was appointed Boundary Commissioner.

The Mexican Surveyor was equally well equipped for his task. José Salazar Larregui (sometimes written José Salazar y Larregui, José Salazar Ilarregui, or José Salazar Ylarregui) was born

[12]For a summary of this work, see Pedro García Conde, *Ensayo estadistica sobre el Estado de Chihuahua* (Chihuahua: Imprenta del Gobierno a Cargo de C. Ramos, 1842).

in Hermosillo, Sonora, in 1823. He studied at the Colegio de Minera and worked as an engineer previous to 1849 and his appointment to the Mexican Boundary Commission.[13]

General Conde apologized for the delay occasioned by his tardiness. He stated that he had left Mexico City on April 18, believing that he had more than enough time to arrive in San Diego by that appointed date. However, like the Americans, he had been delayed by the gold rush. Finally he had secured berths for himself, Salazar, two first class engineers, two second class engineers, and his interpreters on the *Caroline,* which sailed from San Blas on June 24.

On July 6, three days after the arrival of the Mexicans, the Joint Boundary Commission met at the office which Weller had secured in San Diego. Following a reciprocal examination of credentials, the two Commissioners and Surveyors agreed that the Joint Commission could be organized pursuant to the provisions of the Treaty of Guadalupe Hidalgo. Hiram H. Robinson was named secretary for the United States Commission and F. M. Cherero for Mexico. Weller then introduced D. Gahagan as translator and interpreter for the United States, and Conde introduced the Mexican counterpart, Philipe de T. Iturbide, son of the ex-Mexican emperor Agustín de Iturbide. Almost a year and a half after the Treaty of Guadalupe Hidalgo had been signed, Mexico and the United States were ready to survey and mark the boundary. Little did those gentlemen at San Diego realize the difficulties that lay ahead before the task would be completed.

[13]The Mexican Commissioner received his instructions on March 20, 1849. For a copy of these instructions, see Humberto Escoto Ochoa, *Integración y Desintegración de Nuestra Frontera Norte* (Mexico City: 1949), 119-120.

Confluence of the Gila and Colorado Rivers

— *By Charles Shuchard, from* The A. B. Gray Report.

THE CALIFORNIA BOUNDARY

AFTER THE Joint Boundary Commission was formally organized on July 6, 1849, it had first to establish a method of procedure for the survey. Article V of the Treaty of Guadalupe Hidalgo stated that the boundary between Upper and Lower California would begin one marine league south of the harbor of San Diego, "according to the plan of said port, made in the year 1782 by Don Juan Pantoja," then would run in a straight line to the juncture of the Gila and Colorado rivers. At the second meeting of the Commission, held on July 7, it was agreed that the surveyors should report a plan to ascertain the initial point on the boundary of the Pacific Coast and the mode of surveying the line across to the Colorado. By Monday morning, July 9, the surveyors had decided on their methods. They reported that each party would proceed when ready to make the necessary surveys, using its own methods; then the two would meet and work out any differences, after which the actual running and marking would commence. The monuments would be placed afterwards.[1]

[1]Journal of the Joint Boundary Commission, July 6, 7, 9, 1849, *Senate Executive Document* 119, 32 Cong., 1 Sess., 56-58. Hereafter cited as *SED* 119.

Major Emory organized his detachment into three parts. The first party, under his personal direction, established an observatory just south of San Diego, naming it Camp Riley in honor of the commanding general in California; from this point Emory made the observations necessary to determining the longitude and latitude of the initial point on the Pacific Coast. The second surveying party, under the command of Lieutenant Whipple, was sent to the mouth of the Colorado River, escorted by dragoons under the command of Lieutenant Cave J. Couts. Whipple had orders to map the area where the two rivers joined and to determine the exact longitude and latitude at that point. Captain Hardcastle, protected by a detachment of infantry under command of Captain Hayden, was sent with the third surveying party to reconnoiter the 145 miles of country between the two extremities of the California boundary and to select elevated points at which both ends of the line could be sighted directly. Emory had chosen a unique method for drawing the line dividing Upper and Lower California; gunpowder would be ignited at set intervals at each end of the line, and from the points of elevation sightings would be taken that would enable Emory to prepare an accurate map showing the latitude and longitude of the boundary at any given point.[2] Gray, in the meantime, was making a new map of the harbor at San Diego, assisted by Surveyor Salazar.

Emory had no difficulty with his task, nor did Captain Hardcastle. But Lieutenant Whipple, escorted by Couts and the dragoons, ran into a multitude of problems. First they suffered extreme hardships from want of water in reaching the confluence of the Gila and Colorado rivers. Bringing their supplies and equipment in wagons proved extremely difficult during the dry

[2]Emory, *Report,* 4.

season, for their mules almost died of thirst on several occasions. And at every step they were besieged by suffering parties of Argonauts; the Forty-Niners were in full march across the Gila Trail, as the Southwestern route came to be known, and many of them were hungry or lost — or both. Lieutenant Couts in his diary of this expedition commented on the many vexations that resulted:

Oh God! when will I get out of this snap, trouble vexation, pain, suffering and annoyance, from North, South, East and West . . . . This is the first leisure hour, now 10 at night, that I have had since the 12th and there is now a multitude of women and children, on the opposite bank, sending me word that they would be over to see me tomorrow! Though messing by myself, this evening was the first meal eaten alone for some two weeks. My table admits of but three seats, and upon several occasions, I have not got in before the 4th table, very frequently having to keep it set from three p.m., until eight or nine o'clock at night, and then direct the cook to say that the provisions are out, and that the commissary Sergt. is absent. From the way they shovel down the pork and bread, is sufficient proof of its rarity, and sugar and coffee! Some are worse than ratholes to fill.[3]

Another annoyance was the many requests for maps which the pilgrims made of Couts: "They . . . are willing to keep me talking and making way-bills for them from sun-up until sun-down and from sun-down to sun-up. In addition to this they beg me for rations day in and day out. Poor Whipple! Times are hard

[3]Cave J. Couts, *From San Diego to the Colorado in 1849: the Journal and Maps of Cave J. Couts,* ed. by Willian McPherson (Los Angeles: The Zamorano Club, 1932), 48-49. This short work contains an excellent account of the difficulties of the Whipple party, especially those relating to the gold-seekers. Whipple also kept his account; see "Report of the Secretary of War," January 31, 1851, *Senate Executive Document* 19, 31 Cong., 2 Sess.; reprinted as A. W. Whipple, *The Whipple Report,* ed. by E. I. Edwards (Los Angeles: Westernlore Press, 1961). To place this expedition to the Yuma area in proper perspective, see Arthur Woodward, *Feud on the Colorado* (Los Angeles: Westernlore Press, 1955).

on him (?) Ambulance, Umbrella. Oh My!" Apparently there was no love lost between the two lieutenants, for Whipple was extremely concerned that Couts should get no credit for the survey at the mouth of the Gila.

And that survey proved difficult. Once Whipple determined the juncture of the Gila and Colorado rivers and surveyed it, he found that running a straight line to the initial point on the Pacific Coast would give the United States a small amount of land south of the Colorado River. The river turned west and slightly north just past its junction with the Gila, and a half-moon shaped area of land would thus become part of the United States. Still later this same area would become a point of contention between Arizona and California, for in 1850 when California was admitted as a state its southeastern boundary was stipulated as the Colorado River to its confluence with the Gila and then west to a point one marine league south of San Diego. Arizona claimed the portion below the Colorado — but never received it. Another quarrel resulted between Arizona and California over taxes in the same general area. All land south and east of the line established by the Treaty of Guadalupe Hidalgo was considered in the Gila and Salt River Base and Meridian, while all land north and west of the line was in the San Bernardino Base and Meridian. After California was admitted as a state, its county of San Diego extended to the Colorado River, and annually tax collectors from San Diego would visit Yuma, Arizona, and collect taxes on the lands within the San Bernardino Base and Meridian. Eventually a group of irate taxpayers by force of arms prevented the California tax collectors from crossing the river, and from then forward the area was taxed by

Arizona. When Arizona was admitted to the Union as a state, its western boundary was set at the Colorado River, thus ending the dispute.

While these surveys were in progress in the field, events were transpiring elsewhere that would disrupt the work. The national election of 1848 had seen the Democrats losing to the Whigs. While the American Boundary Commission was still in transit to Panama, the administration of Zachary Taylor had taken office. As was customary in those days of political spoilsmanship, Democrats were turned out of office wholesale and replaced by Whig party faithfuls. Unfortunately for John B. Weller — and for the boundary survey — his job was political, and the Whigs wanted it. They were very angry that the appointment of a Boundary Commissioner had not been withheld until after their administration had assumed office.

On June 20, 1849, even before the Joint Boundary Commission had met for the first time in San Diego, the new Secretary of State, John M. Clayton, wrote John Charles Frémont: "The President having thought proper to appoint you the commissioner on the part of the United States for running and marking the boundary line under the fifth article of the treaty of Guadalupe Hidalgo, I transmit your commission in that character." The secretary apparently expected Frémont to fire most of the other members of the Boundary Commission, for he wrote: "You will also forward to this department a full list of the persons (other than military or naval) in the service of the commission on our part . . . ."[4]

Apparently seeking some justification for firing Weller, Clayton wrote the Commissioner on June 26, "It is to be regretted

[4]Clayton to John C. Frémont, Washington, June 20, 1849, *SED* 34, Part I, 9.

that you should have omitted to comply with that part of your instructions which requires you to furnish the department with a list of the persons employed to assist you in the discharge of your duties."[5] This communication, which officially notified Weller of his removal from office, was sent to Frémont with orders that the new Commissioner not deliver the note to Weller unless Frémont not only accepted the post but also took up his work in the field.[6]

On July 20 Secretary Clayton took a step that would hamper Weller completely in the discharge of his duties — he ordered that no further drafts from the Boundary Commissioner be paid.[7] Actually, no money was paid by the Treasury Department for bills signed by Weller after July 1. Weller had already run short of funds at San Diego, however. The costly layover at Panama City and the expenses of transporting the Boundary Commission to San Diego had eaten away the $33,000 that he had drawn in Washington and had taken with him. He could not find merchants in San Diego willing to take his drafts on the treasury; therefore he felt it necessary to go north to Monterey to plead with General Riley for sufficient money to continue the survey until more funds were sent from Washington.

By a stroke of great irony, Weller boarded the *Panama* for his northward trip, a ship carrying Lieutenant Edward Fitzgerald Beale. Secretary Clayton had chosen Beale to carry Frémont's letter of appointment west — the same letter that contained Weller's dismissal. Beale disembarked at Monterey in order to

[5]Clayton to Weller, Washington, June 26, 1849, *ibid.*, 9. Just two days later, on June 28, Clayton wrote that he had received the list of persons working on the Commission on June 27th. See Clayton to Weller, Washington, June 28, 1849, *ibid.*, 10.

[6]Clayton to Frémont, Washington, June 28, 1849, *ibid.*, 10.

[7]Clayton to C. L. Weller, Washington, July 20, 1849, *ibid.*, 11.

see Frémont at San Jose, but Weller decided at the last moment to proceed to San Francisco and try to raise money from the merchants there. Frémont was delighted with the appointment, and in a letter dated August, 1849, wrote his acceptance. The Pathfinder, who has been more appropriately dubbed by some the Great Pathfollower, was still smarting from his court martial and subsequent resignation from the army for his conduct during the Mexican War. He saw this appointment as a vindication. To Secretary Clayton he wrote: "I feel much gratified in accepting the appointment, and beg to offer through you to the President my acknowledgments for the mark of confidence bestowed upon me, and which he may be assured is fully appreciated."[8] Privately he stated: "I regarded the commission as a disavowal on the part of the President of the proceedings recently held against me. Respect to the President, together with a full appreciation of the consideration which had induced him to make the appointment, did not, in my judgment, permit me to decline, and I accordingly accepted the commission, with the intention which I then expressed to Mr. Beale and others, shortly afterwards to resign."[9]

Frémont went at once in search of Weller, finding him at Monterey where General Riley had just refused the Commissioner's request for money. Frémont informed Weller of the change ordered, but did not show the Commissioner the enclosure — thus carrying out Clayton's instructions. Weller poured out his troubles to the Great Pathfinder, painting so black a picture — yet a true one — of the conditions in San Diego that

[8]Frémont to Clayton, Pueblo of San Jose, August, 1849, *ibid.*, 28.

[9]Jesse Benton Frémont Manuscript, Bancroft Library, University of California, as quoted in Lewis B. Lesley, "The International Boundary Survey from San Diego to the Gila River, 1849-1850," *Quarterly of the California Historical Society,* IX (March 1930), 7.

Frémont decided against accepting the appointment. Instead he helped Weller negotiate a draft on the government for $10,000 from San Francisco merchants. Shortly thereafter, Frémont officially resigned as Commissioner, choosing to concentrate on a seat in the United States Senate that seemed within his grasp.[10] Thus Weller continued to function, albeit ineffectively, as head of the Boundary Commission, and the work proceeded.

In September news of Weller's removal arrived at San Diego. The Commissioner was still absent in San Francisco, thus doubling the natural uncertainty that resulted. About the same time at San Diego came verified reports of the amount of wealth that was being picked up by miners at the gold fields. Suddenly the wages of common laborers employed at San Diego rose to $150 per month. Skilled workers did much better; carpenters, for example, demanded and received $10 per day. The price of food rose proportionately, and the soldiers of the escort found themselves forced to pay $1.50 a day for food when their allowance was only twenty cents a day. Such inflation, coupled with the fact that no one on the Commission had been paid for some

[10] Frémont subsequently won this seat, although he drew the short term and thus served only from December 1850, to March 1851. See *ibid.,* 8, especially note 33. Because of this decision Frémont never showed Weller the letter of dismissal, dated June 26, 1849, from Clayton. Later the Secretary of State implied that the letter of dismissal had been sent to Weller through the mail and thus he knew all about this action. On March 1, 1850, Weller wrote sarcastically from San Francisco: "The letter. . . from the Secretary of State, under date 26th June, has never been received [by me]. Diligent search has been made for it in the post office here, but it cannot be found. It may have been directed in the same way that his communication of the 15th March was directed, (San Diego, *Mexico*;) and if so, its failure to reach me is easily accounted for. A little knowledge of the geography of the country oftentimes facilitates the transmission of letters." Weller to Thomas Ewing (Secretary of the Interior), San Francisco, March 1, 1850, *SED* 119, pp. 74-76. See also the Senate hearings relating to this dismissal contained in *Congressional Globe,* 31 Cong., 2 Sess., 78-84. The conclusion was inescapable that Weller's dismissal was entirely political.

time, apparently was more than many of the soldiers and civil employees could bear, especially when gold seemingly could be picked up easily just a few hundred miles to the north. One by one the soldiers began deserting, and one by one the civil employees began resigning. Major Emory later wrote of this period:

> I find no fault with any gentleman in civil life who left the commission at this time. Had I not been an officer of the army in command of troops, and in charge of an important work co-operating with a foreign commission, I should have undoubtedly exercised the privilege of withdrawing.... In this dilemma I did not hesitate to take the responsibility for using the military power in my hands to keep the work from being abandoned. I directed the quartermaster and commissary of the army attached to the escort to furnish supplies and transportation, and I engaged to give each soldier, with the assent of his captain, when not on military duty, two dollars for each day's work done in running the boundary.[11]

This bold action by Emory, subsequently approved by the army, doubtless held the Commission together. It supplied his surveying parties with the necessary labor, and it kept the soldiers sufficiently contented to stop desertions. Later Emory was complimented in orders by the commanding general in California for the successful manner in which his troops were kept from deserting. Yet Emory was despairing of a work so bound up in politics. On September 15 he wrote the Secretary of State, "I now desire, for reasons which, in my judgment, form an insurmountable obstacle to the proper performance of these duties, to be released from all duty with this commission." He did agree to stay with the Commission until the completion of the survey of the California boundary.[12]

Early in October Weller returned to San Diego, and on the 10th of that month the Joint Boundary Commission met formally

[11]Emory, *Report,* 6.

[12]Emory to Clayton, Camp Riley, California, September 15, 1849, *SED* 34, Part I, 28-29.

at the initial point one marine league south of San Diego. Gray and Salazar had completed their work of surveying the harbor of San Diego. Once that was done, they had only to mark off one marine league south to have the initial point on the Pacific; however, since there was no accepted definition of the length of a marine league, they had compromised at 5,564.6 meters. At that point the Joint Commission deposited a written statement, in both Spanish and English, in a hermetically sealed bottle and buried it in the ground; this statement was the agreement of the two commissioners and surveyors that 32° 31′ 59.58″ was the initial point as agreed upon at Guadalupe Hidalgo. A temporary monument was erected at the spot, a more permanent marker to be placed there later.[13]

For the next four months, using army laborers, the work of the survey proceeded smoothly. The success of this operation required the most accurate and elaborate observations; an error of only a few seconds in latitude or longitude at either extremity would have produced a great departure from the true boundary and would have necessitated a new survey. In this operation Emory received little or no help from the Mexican Commission, for although both Salazar and Conde were competent engineers their instruments were so inferior as to be practically useless.[14] Actually, the Mexican Commission was having as much difficulty with its central government as was the American party. General Conde was then using personal funds to pay his em-

[13]Journal of the Joint Boundary Commission, October 10, 1849, *SED* 119, p. 59.

[14]Emory, *Report*, 5. See also José Salazar Ylarregui, *Datos de los trabajos astronomicos y topograficos despuestos en forma de diario. Practicados durante el año de 1849 y principio de 1850 por la Comision de limites Mexicana en la linea que divide esta republica de la de los Estados-Unidos . . .* (Mexico, 1850), 13.

ployees in order that the project not be abandoned and his government embarrassed.[15]

During these four months no funds were forthcoming from Washington, but the members of the Commission showed the same determination as voiced by Major Emory when he wrote: "The outrage inflicted on the commission by withholding funds, and attempting to place at its head persons under influences avowedly hostile, so far from shaking my interest in the great scientific work which I had commenced, only increased my determination to complete it."[16] The work was not carried out harmoniously, however. Gray and Weller became involved in a dispute over jurisdiction that never was resolved fully.[17]

Finally the task was completed. Emory's plan to determine the boundary had worked unbelievably well. The Mexican Commission had accepted his figures without correction; and when the work was put to the test of actual surveying by two parties, one pushing east from San Diego and the other coming west from the Colorado, they met within inches of one another — an error that Emory attributed to the natural inaccuracy of following a straight line over a long distance. The Joint Commission met on January 28, 1850, and agreed that the line had been fixed — that is, that both initial points had been marked and a line run between the two points. All that remained to complete their work was the placing of markers. The following day they agreed that seven monuments would be sufficient; two engineers, one from each party, were to erect these monuments at a later date it was agreed.[18]

[15]Francisco R. Almada, *Diccionario de Historia, Geografia, y Biografía Sonorenses* (Chihuahua City: Ruiz Sandoval, 1952), 298.

[16]Emory, *Report,* 6.

[17]For information on this quarrel, see letters in *SED* 119, 44-49.

[18]Journal of the Joint Boundary Commission, January 28 and 29, 1850, *SED* 119, 60-63.

Only one point of contention arose to mar the harmony of the Joint Boundary Commission's meetings. The survey of the juncture of the Gila and Colorado rivers had shown that the Colorado made a bend northward just past that point, giving the United States approximately three square leagues of land on the south (or left) side of the river. The Mexican Commissioner offered to cede to the United States a corresponding amount of land on the Pacific Coast if the United States would agree to give the land south of the Colorado to Mexico. General Conde reminded Weller that the Joint Commission had within its power the right to make binding agreements concerning the boundary. However, Weller replied that he could not make the agreement; instead, he suggested that the matter be left to the decision of their respective governments.[19]

On February 15, 1850, the Joint Commission held its last formal meeting on the Pacific Coast. Nothing remained to be done on the Pacific Coast side of the boundary except the erecting of the monuments, and a survey of the Gila seemed inadvisable at that time. Supplies at San Diego were too expensive, the Indians were reported hostile in Arizona, and the nearby gold mines were very attractive to employees of the Commission. Therefore the Commissioners agreed to adjourn to meet at El Paso del Norte[20] on the first Monday in November of 1850. They further agreed that should either party fail to meet at the time and place stated, "the one present should commence its operations and push them forward as far as practicable, subject, of course, to the examination and revision of the other party."[21]

[19] *Ibid.*, 61.

[20] This was not the present El Paso, Texas, but the modern Juarez, Chihuahua.

[21] Journal of the Joint Boundary Commission, February 15, 1850, *SED* 119, p. 65.

Again, while progress was being made in the field, political pressures were brought to bear, this time of a very drastic nature. In December of 1849 the overall direction of the boundary survey was transferred from the State Department to the Department of the Interior; in other words, this meant that control of the survey was shifted from John M. Clayton to Thomas Ewing, and Ewing was far more partisan in his political attitudes than Clayton. On December 19, Secretary Ewing addressed a letter to Weller in which he stated:

The direction of the commission for running and marking the boundary line between the United States and Mexico having been transferred to this department, I have to inform you, in case, on the receipt of this, Colonel Frémont shall not have entered upon duty as your successor, that your services are no longer required in said commission; and to request that you will immediately turn over to Major W. H. Emory all the books, papers, and other property in your possession belonging to the United States . . . .[22]

A copy of this letter was sent to Emory, along with orders to take charge of the survey and push it forward to completion as soon as possible.[23]

In taking this action Ewing sought to blacken Weller's reputation as much as possible. Weller was declared a defaulter — *i.e.,* it was said that he had overdrawn on the $50,000 allotted for the boundary survey and thus was personally liable for the drafts he had signed. The $10,000 note he had signed in San Francisco was refused, and his property in California was seized. A later accounting proved, however, that he had spent only $48,936.37, leaving a balance in his account. Furthermore, a note attached to the auditor's report stated: "As Congress had not yet fixed any specific rate for either the commissioner or the

[22]Ewing to Weller, Washington, December 19, 1849, *SED* 34, Part I, 15.
[23]Ewing to Emory, Washington, December 19, 1849, *ibid.,* 15.

surveyor, no salary appears to have been charged in his [Weller's] account for either . . . ."[24] Few public servants of the United States before or since Weller have shown a high regard for their duty as to work more than a year with no idea of what their salaries would be!

Weller replied to Ewing's letter on March 1, 1850, from San Francisco. In this defense of his actions he stated, and correctly, that the Boundary Commission had performed almost Herculean labors under adverse circumstances. "Other parties have been sent into California upon public service," he wrote, "and I challenge a comparison between their labors, their expenses, and those of the boundary commission." He noted that most other phases of public endeavor had been disrupted by the gold rush, but that the survey had progressed nonetheless. "For myself," he concluded, "I am content to await the action of Congress, confident that that branch of the government will in the end do me justice."[25] Weller stayed in San Francisco; there he engaged in private law practice in partnership with James McHall Jones. On January 28, 1851, he was elected by the state legislature to the United States Senate as a Union Democrat; this must have given him considerable satisfaction for he replaced John Charles Frémont, who had been elected to the Senate as a Whig when California was admitted as a state and who had drawn the short term. Weller took office on March 4, 1851, and used his position to become a bitter critic of subsequent work of the Boundary Commission.

Soon after naming Emory acting Commissioner to complete the survey of the boundary between Upper and Lower Califor-

[24] "John B. Weller, United States Commissioner for running the Mexican Boundary, in account with the United States," *ibid.*, Part II, 22.

[25] Weller to Ewing, San Francisco, March 1, 1850, *SED*, 74-76.

nia, Secretary Ewing sent the major additional instructions. Ewing ordered that the total number of employees be "reduced to the lowest number consistent with the proper, though economical, management of the business confided to you." Emory was then to furnish the secretary with a list of all persons employed by Weller, the names of those discharged in the interest of economy, and a list of those still working for the Commission after the reorganization.[26]

Emory received the order to take charge of the survey as temporary Commissioner on February 22, 1850, and reluctantly accepted the post. General Conde immediately addressed a note to the major, stating, "It has afforded me much pleasure, than on the separation of my good friend, Mr. John B. Weller, from the commission, his trust should have devolved upon a person so worthy as yourself . . . ."[27]

With his characteristic energy and directness, Emory proceeded with the work ordered by Secretary Ewing. Immediately he reorganized the Commission and made arrangements for the continuation of the running and marking of the line. Captain Hardcastle was designated to carry out the work of erecting the monuments which the Joint Commission had ordered placed, and Emory began the work of collecting the data he would need to complete a formal report of the California boundary. He reported that he was without funds of any kind, but was moving ahead with the work. Ewing on April 10 approved what Emory had done, and he promised to send funds by the next steamer. However, no money was sent, despite the fact that Congress made a deficiency appropriation of $50,000 to complete this part of the survey.

[26]Ewing to Emory, January 8 and 9, 1850, *SED* 34, Part I, 17-18.
[27]Conde to Emory, San Diego, February 22, 1850, *ibid.*, Part II, 7.

Monument Number One on the Pacific

— *From Senate Doc. 247, 55 Cong., 2 Sess., Part 2, page 173.*

Emory thereupon called the members of the Boundary Commission together and informed them of all that had transpired since he took command. He said he was taking a boat for Washington where he could plead their case, and that he would try to send funds as soon as possible to pay them for their labor and for their travel to their homes. He left Captain Hardcastle in command of the work at that point, and ordered Lieutenant Whipple to take the surveying instruments of the Commission to El Paso by ship. Whipple did this, going by way of Panama, New Orleans, and Indianola, Texas, then pushing overland westward. Had Emory not directed this action, the Boundary Commission would have been entirely without instruments when it arrived at El Paso to keep the rendezvous with the Mexican Commission.

Conde and Salazar likewise left San Diego for El Paso, going by ship to Guaymas, then overland to Mexico City and northward by road. Emory and Gray arrived in New York on November 4, 1850. Emory was relieved of further connection with the boundary survey, much to his satisfaction; he was ordered by Alexander H. H. Stuart, Secretary of the Interior, to turn over all astronomical and surveying instruments to his successor as chief astronomer with the Boundary Commission. Emory did convince Stuart to keep Dr. Charles C. Parry with the Commission, and he persuaded the secretary to send funds to Captain Hardcastle so that the marking of the California boundary could be completed. Hardcastle did finish the job, and reported in Washington in September of 1851.

Surveyor Gray was ordered by Stuart to go immediately to El Paso and resume his duties in the field with the Boundary Commission. This order was not especially pleasing to Gray, for he and Emory had learned upon their arrival in Washington that difficulties were being experienced at El Paso under the direction of the new Boundary Commissioner, John Russell Bartlett.

IV

GETTING TO EL PASO

On October 5, 1850, west of the German settlement of Fredericksburg, Texas, John Russell Bartlett met his first wild Indian. Traveling on the San Antonio-El Paso Road, the newly appointed United States Boundary Commissioner was greeted by Chipota, a fat Lipan Apache chief of some sixty winters. Bartlett received the savage warmly, but was rudely shocked to discover that the chief primarily was interested in only one thing — a drink of whiskey. The offering of a cup of cheer was the standard mode of greeting on the Plains when white man met Redman. The New England gentleman truthfully replied that he had no alcoholic beverages, but the Indian naturally was unconvinced; the Indians believed that all Americans carried firewater with them. Early the next morning, after spending a cold night sleeping on the ground, Chipota rapped on the windows of Bartlett's sumptuous carriage and chattered through his teeth, "*Mucho frio — poco de viskey.*" Bartlett gave him a cup of coffee. As a result the chief went away very disappointed and would not sell sorely needed mules to the Americans.

In this chance encounter Bartlett displayed both his ignorance about the West and his ineptitude in human relations. Not only was he unaware of the true nature of the West and the Indians — he was a firm believer in the "noble redman" concept— but he also was incapable of persuasion or of leading frontier types. These weaknesses in large measure account for the failure of the boundary survey under his direction as Commissioner, a post for which he had no qualification except political connections.

John Russell Bartlett was born in Providence, Rhode Island, on October 23, 1805, but shortly thereafter his parents moved to Kingston, Upper Canada, where they lived until their son was eighteen. He was educated in the schools of Kingston, at Lowville Academy in upstate New York, and in Montreal. His schooling taught him to write a good hand, to be an accountant, and to assist his father in business. He also learned to love good books, acquiring a taste for history and geography which gave his writing a somewhat romantic turn. In addition to these accomplishments, he was also an artist of above-average competence. In 1824, at the age of eighteen, Bartlett returned to Providence where he clerked in the dry goods store of his maternal uncle, William Russell. Four years later he became a bookkeeper in the Bank of North America, likewise a Providence firm, and in 1831 he was named a cashier of the Globe Bank there. During this period he maintained his academic ties by joining the Franklin Society, the Rhode Island Historical Society, and the Providence Athenaeum. In fact, he and his friends, Doctors F. A. Farley and Thomas H. Webb, were regarded as the founders of the latter organization.

In 1834 came one of those chance occurrences which change the course of a life. That year Professor C. C. Rafn of the Royal

Society of Northern Antiquaries of Copenhagen, Denmark, sent a request to the Rhode Island Historical Society for information about the inscriptions on Dighton Rock in nearby Massachusetts. Rafn hoped to prove these inscriptions were Norse. Bartlett was appointed to a committee to investigate the rock, along with his friend Dr. Webb. Drawings of the inscriptions were prepared by these two and sent to Professor Rafn. These sketches were published in *Antiquitates Americanae,* the journal of the Northern Society, and Bartlett and Webb were made honorary members of the organization. This experience introduced Bartlett to the study of the American Indians and interested him in ethnology, for the drawings proved to be the work of American natives and not seafaring Norsemen. Bartlett also maintained an extended correspondence with Rafn, with whom he developed a friendship by mail that probably later inspired him to seek the post of minister to Denmark.

Bartlett moved to New York in 1836 to work for a dry goods commission house, but soon quit that to go into the book-selling business with Charles Welford. Under the name Bartlett and Welford, they imported foreign books for sale, along with American publications, and their store soon became a favorite gathering place for the leading scholars and literary figures of that city. Bartlett joined the New York Historical Society and became its corresponding secretary, a post that brought him an introduction to and close association with Albert Gallatin, the secretary of the treasury under Presidents Jefferson and Madison. With Gallatin, Bartlett founded the American Ethnological Society in 1842, and he prepared and read learned papers before the two groups. In addition, he aided several scholars, including E. G. Squier and John L. Stephens, in their researches, and he is credited with interesting these two men in Central America, both of whom started the study of Mayan archaeology.

It was while in the book business in New York that Bartlett gained some literary fame for his own writings. In 1847 he published *Progress of Ethnology,* an account of the recent studies on that subject throughout the world. The following year his *Dictionary of Americanisms* appeared, which went through four editions by 1878 and which was translated into several foreign languages. Then in 1849 came *Reminiscences of Albert Gallatin,* the result of his association with that well-known figure.

Despite his growing reputation in the literary and scholarly world, however, Bartlett found it increasingly difficult to support his wife, whom he had married in 1831, and their four children. Therefore in 1849 he returned to Providence and began casting about for a new source of income. The Whigs, the party to which he belonged, had won the election of 1848, and he decided to offer his services to the federal government. Possibly because his friend Gallatin had been a member of the diplomatic corps, possibly because of his friendship with Professor Rafn, he wanted an appointment as minister to Denmark. In 1849 he journeyed to Washington armed with a letter of recommendation from Gallatin to John C. Calhoun, the venerable and influential senator from South Carolina, who in turn introduced him to Senators Jefferson Davis of Mississippi and Thomas Hart Benton of Missouri. He also secured the support of the "Little Giant," Stephen A. Douglas of Illinois. Yet despite this backing from powerful Democrats and despite his Whig connections, Bartlett failed in his quest for the Danish post. It went to another man.

Dame Fortune and his political friends had not entirely forgotten Bartlett, however. Just at that critical point in his life, the position of United States Boundary Commissioner was offered to him. He accepted the post, according to his own statement, because he had led a sedentary life and wanted to travel for a change. It also offered him a chance to see for himself the object of his long admiration and interest, the American Indian. Therefore, despite his ignorance of the wiles of diplomacy and his obvious lack of qualifications to command a survey through wild and inhospitable country, he accepted the proffered post.

Along with his certificate of appointment as Commissioner, dated June 15, 1850, came orders directing him, during the course of the survey, to collect information on the possible construction of a road, canal, or railway through the area, as provided by Article VI of the Treaty of Guadalupe Hidalgo; to seek knowledge of quicksilver, precious metals, ores, and other valuable substances; to look for a more practicable route to California for immigrants; and to keep full records and make a map of the country traversed. For his services he was to receive three thousand dollars a year, plus expenses.[1]

This appointment eased Bartlett's financial problems, but it brought him no respite from troubles. Hundreds of applications poured in from young men interested in the adventure they imagined would be involved — they wanted "to see the elephant," as the saying went at that time. Many of these applications were endorsed by influential Whig Congressmen and Senators, and Bartlett was too inexperienced to resist such pressures. Thus many employees of the new Boundary Commission were hired because of their political connections rather than for their knowledge and experience — young men such as Edward C. Clarke, son of Senator John H. Clarke of Rhode Island.

[1]D. C. Goddard (Secretary of the Interior *ad interim*) to Bartlett, Washington, August 1, 1850, *SED* 119, pp. 87-89.

Not all the hiring of incompetent personnel was the result of outside pressures, however, for the Commissioner hired his own brother, George F. Bartlett, as commissary for the expedition at $1,500 per year.

Among Bartlett's best choices for personnel were his old friend Dr. Thomas H. Webb, hired as surgeon and secretary, and John C. Cremony, a reporter with the *Boston Herald* who was retained as an interpreter because of his previous experience in the area to be traversed. And there were some of the young gentlemen who later would become famous in their own right—such as seventeen-year-old Frank Wheaton, who was employed as "chain-bearer and station-marker." A native of Providence, Rhode Island, and a nephew of the famed jurist and diplomat Henry Wheaton, the lad would serve five years with the Boundary Commission, then accept a commission in the army. During the Civil War he rose to the rank of brigadier general of volunteers; after that conflict he fought in the Indian Wars, gaining fame for his successful pursuit of the Modoc Indians in 1872. He retired as a major general in 1897.

Finally the task of selecting personnel was completed by Bartlett — one hundred and eleven civilians and a military escort of eighty-five men of the 3rd Infantry, commanded by Lieutenant Colonel Lewis S. Craig. A Virginian, Craig had received an appointment as second lieutenant of dragoons in October of 1837. During the Mexican War he was breveted a major for gallant and meritorious conduct at the battle of Monterrey, and a lieutenant colonel for the same bravery at the battles of Contreras and Churubusco. Craig doubtless would have had a brilliant career in the army, but his life was cut tragically short during the course of the boundary survey.

Besides the selection of personnel from among the many applicants, Bartlett had also to devote himself to securing supplies. Here again the new Commissioner showed his incapacity for office. He assumed that all the astronomical and surveying equipment then in use by the boundary Commission at San Diego would be transported to El Paso for use there, and failed to secure additional or better equipment. Later this omission would cause serious delays from shortages. George F. Bartlett was no more experienced than his brother; he bought mounds of supplies, clothing, and wagons, even four iron boats that could be disassembled. Most of his choices later proved very unsatisfactory.

To supervise the use of the four boats of the Commission, Lieutenant Issac G. Strain of the United States Navy was attached to the group. Strain apparently had joined the wrong branch of the service, for he had visions of the glories of a cavalry charge. He assumed command of the corps of engineers of the Commission, outfitting them in uniforms consisting of blue flannel shirts, dark trousers, and broad-brimmed white felt hats. Strain held drills until he felt that the engineers presented a respectable appearance as a cavalry group.

The reorganized Boundary Commission sailed without its leader aboard the steamer *Galveston,* which was bound for Indianola, Texas, by way of New Orleans, on August 3. Bartlett and a few others sailed ten days later. Aboard the *Galveston* friction quickly developed between military and civilian components of the Commission, and between Lieutenant Strain and Lt. Colonel John McClellan, the Topographical Engineer named to replace Emory as Chief Astronomer. He was very indignant when he discovered that Bartlett had made arrangements for the civilian mechanics to be fed food put in tubs and placed at various points about the deck of the ship. Then at Key West, Florida, Lieutenant Strain led a group of men ashore for a drunken brawl; when they returned to the ship, the lieutenant, who technically was in command of the group while at sea, ordered one man thrown overboard and two others to be tied and then locked in their cabins. McClellan forceably intruded to stop this punishment, thereby incurring the wrath and hatred of Lieutenant Strain. And while the *Galveston* was at New Orleans, the only quarters provided for the civilians was in a house of prostitution,[2] another occurrence which McClellan protested.

On August 30 the *Galveston* docked at Indianola, Texas. There the Commission was beset by still further difficulties. The quartermaster sent in advance of the main party to buy mules, James Myer, had for the most part purchased unbroken and unshod animals. These had to be broken before the expedition could push on to San Antonio, then the largest city in the Lone Star State and the place where Bartlett intended to complete his outfitting. The mules were harnessed to logs, which they hauled about for several days before becoming sufficiently docile to be trusted to the wagons. The harness that Myer had purchased in the East proved too large for the small Mexican mules of Texas, and had to be cut down before being usable. More days were consumed in this process — days which the Commission could ill afford if it was to be in El Paso by the first Monday in November.

On September 6 all was in readiness to start for San Antonio, the town of Victoria some thirty miles away being the first objec-

[2] "Report of the Secretary of the Interior, Communicating . . . a Copy of the Charges Preferred against the Present Commissioner Appointed to Run and Mark the Boundary Line between the United States and Mexico," *SED* 60, 32 Cong., 1 Sess., 52-53.

tive. Bartlett set out in advance in his sumptuous carriage, which was drawn by four fleet mules. The inside of this vehicle, according to John C. Cremony, "was well supplied with Colt's and Sharp's rifles, Colt's pistols, a double-barreled shot gun, lots of ammunition, a spyglass, and a number of small but useful tools."[3] Invariably the Commissioner's traveling companion in this coach was Dr. Webb, and the two Rhode Islanders whiled away the hours trying out their shotguns on "prairie fowl, the great curlew, and flocks of quail." Herds of deer could be seen in the distance, and the young gentlemen of the party dashed out with their weapons to "try their hand at this exciting sport."[4] That first evening out from Indianola the group dined on saddle of venison, and indeed it seemed that they had made the right choice in joining the Boundary Commission. The chase, the bagging of game, and the roasting of venison on a campfire were all things to write home about.

At Victoria the mules had to be shod, a process made doubly slow because the horseshoes purchased in New York were too large for the small Mexican mules of the Southwest. Some of the young gentlemen found themselves sweating and cursing before this task was completed. And at Victoria Colonel McClellan fell ill — or so his servant reported. Bartlett immediately sent Dr. J. M. Bigelow, the surgeon of the Commission, to attend McClellan. Dr. Bigelow returned with a hint that McClellan's sickness was "Barleycorn-itis." McClellan had been born in Pennsylvania in 1805, had graduated from West Point in 1826, and had been breveted a lieutenant colonel for bravery during the Mexican War. He was not related to George B.

[3] John C. Cremony, *Life Among the Apaches* (San Francisco: A. Roman & Company, 1868), 18-19. Reprinted in 1951 by Arizona Silhouettes, Tucson.

[4] Bartlett, *Personal Narrative of Exploration and Incidents . . .* (2 vols., New York, 1854), I, 152. Reprinted in 1965 by the Rio Grande Press.

McClellan, who would win such prominence during the Civil War. McClellan soon recovered sufficiently to move on toward San Antonio, and Bartlett doubtless breathed a prayer of hope that the colonel would restrain his appetite for whiskey.

The trip to San Antonio, where they arrived on September 27, was not made without incident. In fact, during this short trip Bartlett and the young gentlemen of the Commission had their first real introduction to the violence of the frontier. Two days before arriving at San Antonio a Texas teamster known simply as Green, who had been hired at Victoria to drive one of the unruly teams of mules, was out gathering wood for his campfire. Discovering the fence of a Mexican farmer, Green began pulling off pieces of wood. The owner appeared and ordered Green off his property, threatening the Texan with a knife. Green returned to camp, got his pistol, and went for the wood he had been forced to drop. The Mexican was waiting with drawn knife, and began advancing on the Texan. Green walked to within three feet of the Mexican, then calmly drew his revolver and fired, inflicting a mortal wound. Bartlett ordered Green arrested and had him placed in a tent with two men standing guard. That night the prisoner simply lifted the back of the tent, crawled out, and jumped on a nearby horse. He was never found.[5] In fact, none of the Texans would help look for him — in 1850 the Alamo and Goliad were still fresh memories, and killing a Mexican hardly seemed a crime to them.

A second such incident occurred on September 28, the day after the Commission arrived at San Antonio. Another Texan hired as a teamster, a man named Turner, got into a quarrel with a butcher hired in Washington, Mr. Tennant. The butcher was heard to say that he had no fear of the Texan, that he would

[5] *Ibid.*, 32-33.

John R. Bartlett

— Courtesy John Carter Brown Library, Brown University.

lay aside his knife and fight the man fairly. Turner replied that this was agreeable to him, but when Tennant laid aside his weapons the Texan drew a Bowie knife and stabbed the unfortunate Easterner, causing the man to die in half an hour. Turner then calmly sheathed his knife and jumped on a nearby horse, disappearing into the chaparral. Members of the Commission immediately hastened in pursuit of the fugitive and succeeded in capturing him. Bartlett lodged the murderer in San Antonio's jail; he was tried and sentenced to fifteen years imprisonment, but escaped after serving only two years.[6]

In San Antonio the pressing urgency of getting to El Paso caused Bartlett to push ahead with an advance party of thirty men, leaving the rest to make their way westward soon afterward. The trip was actually without incident — although to the Easterners it seemed very adventurous. The party arrived in El Paso on November 13, only to learn that General Conde and the Mexican party had just then reached Chihuahua City.[7] Bartlett sent a runner south with news of his arrival to the Mexican Commissioner, then occupied himself with excursions through the countryside, made in company with the army officers at the American military post of Camp El Paso.[8]

When the remainder of the members of the Commission arrived at El Paso, Bartlett found it necessary to dismiss many

[6] *Ibid.*, 34-36.

[7] Bartlett to M. T. McKennon (Secretary of the Interior), El Paso, November 14, 1850, *SED* 119, pp. 380-384.

[8] What would eventually become Fort Bliss, Texas, was established on September 14, 1849. However, the troops there were withdrawn to Fort Fillmore, New Mexico, on August 17, 1851. The site was regarrisoned on January 11, 1854, and shortly thereafter the name was changed to Fort Bliss. See Francis P. Prucha, S.J., *A Guide to the Military Posts of the United States, 1787-1895* (Madison: State Historical Society of Wisconsin, 1964), 61. The American village which would eventually become El Paso, was then known as Franklin.

men from the government's employ. Many of these, of course, were teamsters who had been hired only for the trip to El Paso, but others were disaffected and disillusioned "young gentlemen" who had been hired in the East. The hardships of the trail had not been as romantic as they had envisioned. Some of those who were discharged returned to San Antonio and made their way home again, but the roughest element congregated at the Texas village of Socorro, a few miles down the Rio Grande from El Paso.

Within a month after the arrival still more of the Commission employees became dissatisfied. On January 6, 1851, a formal complaint was lodged with the Commissioner, bearing the signatures of twenty-six "officers and members of the United States and Mexican boundary commission." It stated:

> . . . We are not properly provided, by the commissary department, with such provisions as are necessary to our comfortable subsistence; that the provisions that are issued are insufficient in quantity and inferior in quality. We were quartered here [San Elizario, Texas] after the arrival of the train on the 9th of December, 1850, since which time rations have been issued three different times, each for ten days' subsistence; . . . rice that is inferior in quality, and we believe would be condemned by a board of survey; pork that we are informed *was* condemned at the military post, and which we unhesitatingly say is unfit for use; flour that we find, on comparison, is much inferior to flour that has been condemned as unfit for use at the military post here, and which we unhesitatingly say is injurious to our health, and not fit to eat. We have received but half rations of rice and half rations of beans. Fresh beef has been issued every third day at Socorro; and we say, with all truth, that not one pound of the beef that we have received since our arrival here was such as should be eaten by man regardful of his life and health.[9]

[9] "A complaint against the commissary on account of the insufficiency and inferiority of provisions," *SED* 119, pp. 42-43.

With considerable heat, prompted no doubt by the fact that the commissary of the Commission was his brother, Bartlett replied that his own table was supplied from the same source as that of the signers of the petition. He stated that he had procured a sample of the flour in question, that bread had been baked with it, and that he "found it excellent." George Bartlett, the commissary, also replied formally to the petitioners: "If you . . . had taken into consideration the great difficulty I have to encounter in procuring supplies, I am convinced that the complaint would never have been made."[10]

Next came a quarrel over pay. Members of the Commission asked Bartlett why they were not getting the salary they believed they had contracted to work for, and the Commissioner passed them along to Jonathan Chamberlin, superintendent of the mechanics. Chamberlin wrote Bartlett a hot note stating:

> Having been informed by the members of the mechanics' corps of the commission that you charge me with altering their pay, after the same was fixed under your order at Indian Point, I have the pleasure to inform you that I have now in my possession the original book from which you copied the list; and you know that you never have mentioned the subject of pay to me since I gave you the list at Indian Point. It would therefore become you more, as commissioner of the United States, to tell these men . . . that the expenses of the expedition had so far exceeded your estimate that it became necessary to curtail the expenses, and that in accordance with the advice of those around you, you had cut down the pay of the mechanics, and not charge me, an humble member of the commission, with the meanest of conduct — *that of deception without an object.*[11]

[10]See Bartlett to J. H. Prioleau, El Paso, January 6, 1851, and George F. Bartlett to Prioleau, Socorro, Texas, January 7, 1851, *SED* 119, pp. 43-46.

[11]Jonathan Chamberlin to Bartlett, San Elizario, Texas, January 19, 1851, *ibid.*, 49-50.

These various quarrels led to some dismissals and some resignations. These men joined the ones already dismissed and at Socorro, with the result that a band of vile-tempered individuals were gathered at the little village — a cauldron boiling with discontent. Violence was bound to break out, and soon it did. By January 29 Quartermaster James Myer was reporting "some slight depredations" at Socorro, and asked for additional guards for the Commission's property.[12] That same night at a dance in the village a group of the "ruffians," as Myer termed them, made their appearance. A quarrel ensued during which Edward C. Clarke, son of Senator John H. Clarke of Rhode Island, and assistant quartermaster with the Commission, was stabbed nine times in the breast and abdomen. Another employee, Charles Gates, was shot in the leg.

Messengers were quickly dispatched to the nearby military authorities with a request for help, but this was denied on the grounds that the altercation was a civil affair. There was no recourse to civil justice, for the sole authority in Socorro was the alcalde, a weak and timid individual. Therefore the law abiding citizens of the town joined with members of the Boundary Commission to form a vigilante group. A systematic search of every house in town yielded eight of the "ruffians." These were taken before a hastily convened court and given a trial. Six jurors were selected from among the Mexican citizens of Socorro and six from the Boundary Commission. A judge and prosecuting attorney were named, but the defendants refused the proffered services of a defense attorney. They were treating the entire proceedings as a joke, feeling that nothing would come of the trial.

During the trial it was feared that other members of the rough set would try to free those captured. Thus the judge sat

[12]Myer to Bartlett, Socorro, Texas, January 29, 1851, *ibid.*, 53.

with a pistol openly displayed, as did the jury and most of the spectators. Two days were taken up with the hearing of evidence, then the prisoners were allowed to speak in their own defense. The jury took only a short time to deliberate before returning a verdict of guilty against William Craig, Marcus Butler, and John Wadel. The judge thereupon pronounced a sentence of death, commenting that he wished the leader of the ruffians, Alexander Young, had also been captured and brought before the court.

The three men were taken immediately to the village plaza. A priest offered to give them consolation, but his services were refused. Butler, the youngest of the three doomed men, broke down and wept aloud, but his two companions told him to act bravely since he could die but once — and should do that one as a man, not as a coward. A cottonwood tree served as a gallows. Ropes were cast over a convenient branch and the three men sent into eternity without delay. The vigilantes then served notice that all unemployed persons in the village would be healthier elsewhere — a warning that was taken by the remaining ruffians within twenty-four hours. Some of the vigilantes went searching for the missing Young, and a few days later he was captured far down the Rio Grande. He was returned to Socorro and tried in the same manner as the other three men — and sentenced to hang. Young made a confession to the priest, then asked to receive a good burial. At 4:30 in the afternoon the same cottonwood that had served his companions was likewise his springboard into eternity.[13]

[13]For the details of these difficulties, see *ibid.*, 53-55; and Carlysle Graham Raht, *The Romance of Davis Mountains and Big Bend Country* (Odessa, Texas: The Rahtsbook Company, 1963), 105-112.

Most of these difficulties of the Boundary Commission came to light later because of still another firing that had occurred. While the Boundary Commission was at San Antonio, Lieutenant Strain had become disgusted and had left the expedition. He hurried to Washington where he filed charges against Colonel McClellan — charges of drunkenness and conduct unbecoming an officer and a gentleman. The Secretary of the Interior wrote an order relieving McClellan from his position with the Commission, but since the colonel had served long years of faithful service (and had powerful political friends) he was to be offered a chance to resign *"on the score of ill health,"* rather than have the official order of removal handed him.[14] McClellan indignantly refused a chance to resign from the commission, demanding instead that he be furnished with "the charges and specifications against me, by whom preferred, and the names and residence of the witnesses to substantiate them."[15] Bartlett could not furnish these; instead he handed the colonel the orders from Washington for McClellan to report to the Department of the Interior.

When McClellan departed, Bartlett was wrong if he breathed a sigh of relief. The colonel did as he was ordered — he reported to Washington — but only because that was the best place to level a series of charges at Commissioner Bartlett. McClellan believed that it was Bartlett who had caused his removal (ironically Bartlett was not the culprit here, but Lieutenant Strain), and he intended to get revenge. McClellan charged Barlett with incompetence; he declared that George F. Bartlett,

[14]Stuart to Bartlett, Washington, October 10, 1850, *SED* 119, p. 94; Bartlett to McClellan, El Paso, December 4, 1850, *ibid.*, 28.

[15]McClellan to Bartlett, San Elizario December 9, 1851 [*sic*—1850], *ibid.*, 28.

the Commissioner's brother, had brought personally owned goods to the frontier at government expense and then had sold them at exorbitant prices to the workers; he charged Bartlett with keeping Quartermaster Myer in that post even though the Commissioner knew Myer to be defrauding the government.

The new Secretary of the Interior, Alexander H. H. Stuart, backed Bartlett as much as he could. He officially removed McClellan from the Boundary Commission, but the colonel was not reprimanded; instead, he was placed in charge of the Tennessee River surveys. Myer was dismissed as quartermaster of the Commission, and George F. Bartlett was transferred to another post.[16] Thus by the time the surveying actually began at El Paso, many of the members of the Commission had been discredited. Bartlett's naivete in hiring and in selecting administrative personnel had almost wrecked the Commission — but he had yet to commit his biggest blunder.

[16]"Report of the Secretary of the Interior," *SED,* 60, 32 Cong., 1 Sess., 3-4, contains McClellan's charges; McClellan's defense of his own conduct is in *ibid.,* 42-43, 51-52. The final disposition of the entire set of charges and countercharges is in "Report of the Secretary of the Interior Made in Compliance with a Resolution of the Senate Calling for Information whether any Steps were Taken to Investigate the Charges Preferred by Col. McClellan against the Commissioner to Run and Mark the Boundary Between the United States and Mexico," *SED* 89, 32 Cong., 1 Sess., 2.

V

THE BARTLETT-CONDE AGREEMENT

ON DECEMBER 1, 1850, General Conde and the Mexican Commission arrived at El Paso del Norte. The following day Conde addressed a note to Bartlett announcing his arrival and readiness to proceed with the survey. The American Commissioner visited his Mexican counterpart two hours later, and they agreed to hold the first formal meeting of the Joint Commission the next day, December 3, at Bartlett's quarters on the north side of the river. Thereafter, they would alternate their meetings on the American and Mexican sides of the Rio Grande.

The first task these two gentlemen set for themselves was establishing the point where the Rio Grande struck the southern boundary of New Mexico. The Treaty of Guadalupe Hidalgo, in tracing this part of the line, stated:

> The Boundary line between the two Republics shall commence in the Gulf of Mexico, three leagues from land, opposite the mouth of the Rio Grande, otherwise called Rio Bravo del Norte . . .; from thence, up the middle of that river, following the deepest channel, where it has more than one, to the point where it strikes the southern boundary of New Mexico (which runs north of the town called *Paso*) to its western termi-

nation; thence northward, along the western line of New Mexico, until it intersects the first branch of the river Gila . . . . The southern and western limits of New Mexico, mentioned in this Article, are those laid down in the Map, entitled *"Map of the United States, as organized and defined by various acts of the Congress of said Republic, and constructed according to the best Authorities. Revised Edition. Published at New York in 1847 by J. Disturnell . . . ."*[1]

Very shortly after the two Commissioners started meeting, however, they discovered two errors in Disturnell's map that would make it difficult to determine where the boundary line struck "the southern boundary of New Mexico." As drawn on the Disturnell map, the line turned west from the Rio Grande at a point on the Rio Grande that was seven minutes of latitude, or eight English miles, north of El Paso [Juarez, Chihuahua] and ran westward for three degrees of longitude, or 175.28 miles, before turning north to strike the nearest branch of the Gila River. But the Disturnell map located El Paso at 32° 15′ north latitude, when the true position was found to be 31° 45′. Moreover, the map showed the point where El Paso was located to be at 104° 39′ west longitude, when its true position was 106° 29′. This error of half a degree in latitude and longitude placed El Paso (on the Disturnell map) thirty-four miles too far north and well over a hundred miles too far east.

The errors in the Disturnell map were easy to account for. The Disturnell map of 1847 was a plagiarism of a map published in 1828, which had been stolen from an imprint in 1826, which was a reproduction of a publication in 1822. That year H. S. Tanner, a map publisher in Philadelphia, issued "A Map of North America, Constructed According to the Latest Information." The map was reprinted in 1826, then stolen by White, Gallaher & White for a map in 1828 entitled "Mapa de los

[1]Malloy, *Treaties*, 1109-1110.

Estados Unidos de Méjico." Disturnell borrowed from the latter to compile his map, which he originally issued in 1846 and which went through twenty-three editions by 1858. The Treaty referred to the Disturnell map of 1847, *"Revised Edition."* There were seven different printings of the map that year, each slightly different from the others. It was the seventh edition that Nicolas P. Trist had with him when he negotiated at Guadalupe Hidalgo.[2] Errors in longitude and latitude, never accurately made at El Paso, were simply carried forward by each map-maker in turn.

The Mexican Commissioner, a trained engineer, quickly discovered the error and brought it to Bartlett's attention. To Conde the solution to the problem of locating the initial point on the Rio Grande was easily solved: the treaty map must be used as it was drawn, regardless of errors. The boundary, therefore, should begin at that point of latitude which was seven minutes north of the indicated location of El Paso — *i.e.,* at 32° 22′, just as shown on the map — even though this would establish the line not eight miles north of El Paso, but forty-two! Further, Conde contended, the line should run west three degrees from the Rio Grande — as shown on the Disturnell map, of course — before turning north to intersect the Gila.[3]

Regarding the Conde proposal, Bartlett wrote the Secretary of the Interior, "This I could not consent to, inasmuch as this point, when placed in its position on a correct map, would give the United States but half a degree of the southern boundary for New Mexico, instead of three degrees . . . ." He declared his belief that the intent of the negotiators at Guadalupe Hidalgo

[2]Hammond (ed.), *Treaty of Guadalupe Hidalgo,* 69-70.

[3]Bartlett to Alexander H. H. Stuart (Secretary of the Interior), El Paso, December 18, 1850, *SED* 119, pp. 386-390.

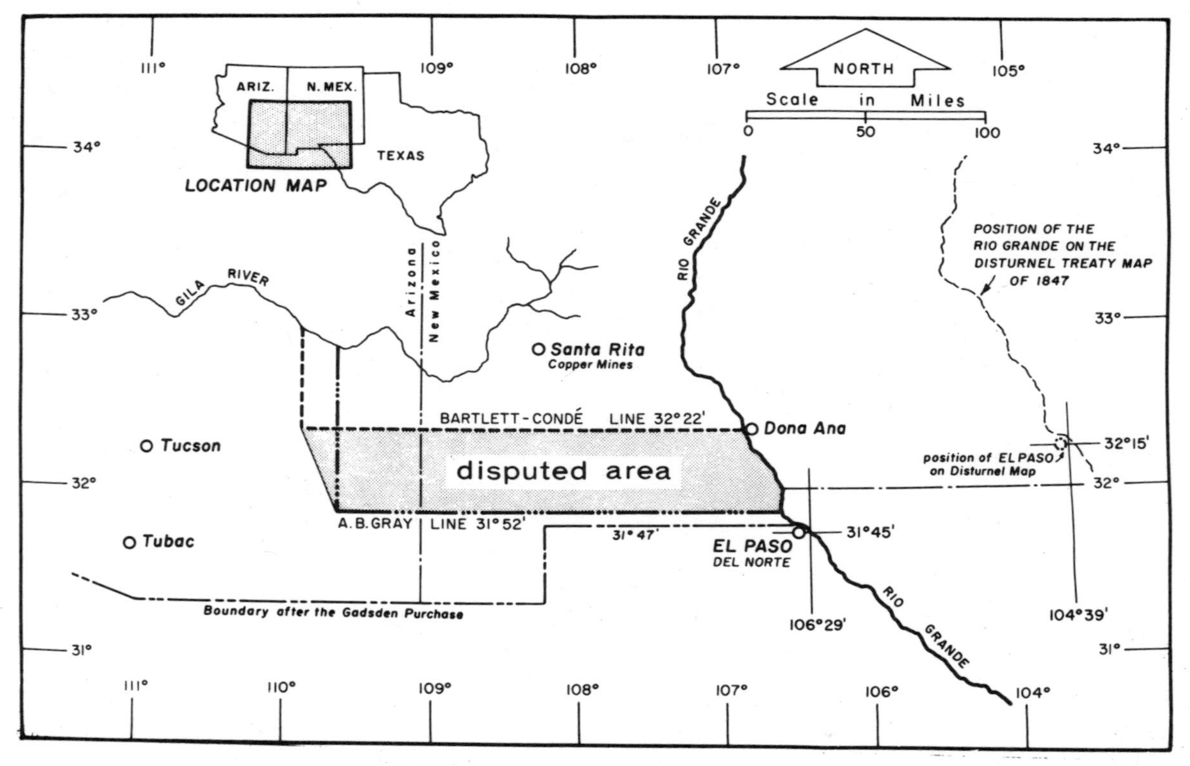

—*Drawn by Don Bufkin.*

had been that the southern boundary of New Mexico should run only sligthly north of El Paso — eight miles to be exact — and indeed the line drawn on the map proved this. The fact that El Paso was "more than thirty miles out of its true position" was delaying the survey, but Bartlett declared that a compromise could be reached since General Conde had evinced "an earnest desire that we should agree."[4]

General Conde immediately addressed a note to the Mexican Secretary of War and Marine and of Relations asking for instructions to guide him in the meetings with Bartlett. The reply from Mexico City was most emphatic: "The parallel [in the Disturnell map] is to be considered absolute relative to [the position of] El Paso del Norte. The pretensions on the part of the Americans [to set the boundary eight miles north of El Paso] are incompatible with the latitude that is given to this parallel in the specifications of the treaty." As to the question of longitude, the Secretary was equally specific: "The western limit of New Mexico is formed by a line that has been impossible to follow on the ground, and which it is supposed passes across the peaks of the Sierra de los Mimbres. For this reason it is necessary that you do not concede this meridian . . . ."[5]

Bartlett turned to the only man with experience in the boundary survey who was actually at El Paso — Lieutenant Whipple. Whipple was serving as acting chief astronomer with the American Commission following the departure of Colonel McClellan. Bartlett asked Whipple to submit a written opinion concerning the error in the Disturnell map, and to suggest therein a solution. Whipple replied that since the boundary had not been laid down in the treaty according to its latitude and longi-

[4]*Ibid.*, 387-88.
[5]Ochoa, *Integración y Desintegración*, 124-125.

tude, the placing of the initial point would be difficult because the Disturnell map was full of "wavering lines." However, because El Paso has been named in the treaty, he thought that the Commissioners should fix the initial point of the town at the distance shown on the map — *i.e.,* seven minutes or eight miles — and then extend the boundary westward three degrees from that point, turning due north there until reaching the Gila.[6] Bartlett included Whipple's analysis in the official papers of the survey, declaring at the time that he was in full agreement with it.[7]

The two Commissioners at their next meeting agreed that each side should present its arguments in writing. Conde, in his statement, expressed a willingness to "adopt a means of fulfilling the will of those who made the treaty," and a compromise was reached on Christmas day, 1850. To satisfy Conde the initial point on the Rio Grande was fixed forty-two miles north of El Paso rather than eight — *i.e.,* at 32° 22′ north latitude, as shown on the Disturnell map, rather than at 31° 52′ as it would have been if the correct latitude of El Paso had been used. To please Bartlett the line was then to run three degrees westward from the Rio Grande — *i.e.,* three degrees west from 106° 29′ west longitude rather than from 104° 39′, the erroneous longitude indicated on the map. From the western point thus determined for the southern boundary of New Mexico, the line would then proceed northward until it reached the nearest branch of the Gila, and run down that river according to the treaty.[8]

[6] Whipple to Bartlett, El Paso, December 28, 1850, *SED* 119, 37.

[7] Bartlett to Whipple, El Paso, December 30, 1850, *ibid.,* 38.

[8] Ochoa, *Integración y Desintegración,* 126; Bartlett to Stuart, El Paso, December 28, 1850, *SED* 119, p. 391; J. Fred Rippy, *The United States and Mexico* (New York, 1931), 109-110.

Bartlett was happy with this compromise. To Secretary Stuart he wrote:

> The happy result . . . is to me a source of very great satisfaction. On arriving here and finding the map of Disturnell so utterly at variance with truth, as far as the position of the Rio Grande, of the town of El Paso, and the limits of New Mexico are concerned, I entertained fears that the joint commission would find it impossible to agree upon a line of boundary which should comply with the treaty.[9]

The American Commissioner believed that Conde would never have agreed to extending the boundary three degrees west from the Rio Grande itself had he not agreed to fixing the initial point on the Rio Grande at 32° 22′. He confided to Secretary Stuart that he had yielded land of no value south of 32° 22′ while gaining for the United States an area to the west which contained copper — and perhaps even gold and silver.[10] Mexicans, however, were not happy with the compromise. Humberto Escoto Ochoa, a scholar who studied diligently in Mexican records about this survey, wrote in 1949: "Ignoring the reasons Conde had for accepting the idea of the American Commissioner, he did not have . . . any basis for acceding to it, for the Mexican position was correct."[11]

Once this compromise had been reached, Conde and Bartlett ordered the surveyors to locate with exactness where the compromise point on the Rio Grande, 32° 22′, actually lay. As the American Surveyor, A. B. Gray, had not yet reached El Paso, Bartlett sent Lieutenant Whipple with Salazar to make this survey. While the two men were thus occupied, a problem arose which threatened to wreck the compromise. By the provisions of the treaty, all business transacted by the Joint Boundary Com-

[9]Bartlett to Stuart, El Paso, December 28, 1850, *SED* 119, p. 391.
[10]Rippy, *The United States and Mexico,* 109-110.
[11]Ochoa, *Integración y Desintegración,* 126.

mission was to be by the unanimous act of the Commissioners *and* Surveyors of both governments. But Gray — being absent — could not sign the agreement. Early in the spring of 1851 General Conde notified Bartlett that he desired to expedite the survey — well he might, for he was paying the Mexican Commission's members out of his own pocket. Conde had already complained to his government about delays caused by the Americans and his government in turn had made formal complaints to Washington. With Conde's concurrence, therefore, Bartlett decided to appoint Lieutenant Whipple Surveyor *ad interim* for the United States so the agreement could be signed.[12]

This action Bartlett felt, was justified because spring was approaching — the best season of the year for engaging in field work in the Southwest. The Commissioner knew that such an appointment could be made only by the government and that he had no authority to assign anyone to the post, even temporarily. In a letter to the Secretary of the Interior in May of 1851, he explained his action and stated his hope that it would meet with departmental approval.[13] Stuart did sanction the appointment of Whipple, and wrote the Secretary of State, Daniel Webster, that the action was necessary because of the "protracted and dangerous illness" of Gray. Lieutenant Whipple was to be recognized as Surveyor *ad interim,* Stuart wrote, and his official acts in that capacity were "to be considered binding" on Gray.[14] Bartlett later allowed his memory to persuade him that Whip-

[12]Barlett to Whipple, In Camp Near the Initial Point, April 23, 1851, *SED* 119, p. 241.

[13]Bartlett to Stuart, Santa Rita del Cobre, May, 1851, *ibid.,* 406-408.

[14]Stuart to Daniel Webster (Secretary of State), Washington, February 11, 1852, *ibid.,* 124-125.

ple's appointment was made "by order of the Secretary of the Interior."[15]

On April 24, 1851, with Whipple acting as Surveyor for the United States, the Joint Boundary Commission formally met with witnesses at the initial point on the Rio Grande (just north of present Las Cruces, New Mexico) and deposited a document in a temporary monument erected at the spot. The document testified that the Commissioners, on behalf of their two nations, "do establish this point on the right bank of the river Bravo or Grande del Norte (32° 22′) . . . which, in accordance with the provisions of the fifth article of said treaty, is 'the point where it strikes the southern boundary of New Mexico.' " The paper was signed by Conde and Bartlett as Commissioners, by Salazar as *Agremensor,* and by Whipple as "Surveyor and Astronomer."[16]

With this major question seemingly settled, all that remained for the Joint Boundary Commission to do was to survey the Rio Grande southward, the southern boundary of New Mexico westward, and the Gila down its course to the Colorado. Bartlett therefore ordered all the surveying parties except one — which was to begin working down the Rio Grande — to move from El Paso to the copper mines at Santa Rita del Cobre,[17] where a camp was established. Colonel Craig, commanding the military escort, had determined to make that place his headquarters until the Joint Commission pushed still farther west. Dr. Webb bor-

[15] Bartlett, *Personal Narrative,* I, 152.

[16] Copy of the document deposited at the initial point on the Rio Grande, *SED* 119, pp. 233-234.

[17] The copper mine at Santa Rita, New Mexico, is one of the oldest known mines in the United States, having been worked by Indians, Spaniards, and Mexicans before the arrival of the Americans in the Southwest. For more of the contemporary comments about Santa Rita, see Rex Arrowsmith, *Mines of the Old Southwest* (Santa Fe: Stagecoach Press, 1963), 29-37.

rowed Bartlett's sumptuous carriage, and in company with John C. Cremony, the interpreter, he set out westward from El Paso. In order not to be bored by the slow travel of the dragoons, Webb invariably ordered his driver to hurry ahead; then they would wait at the appointed campsite for the evening. Cremony rode on horseback, traveling with Webb, as he said, because he would not "leave my party in so dangerous an Indian country as the one we were now penetrating."[18] Thus it was that members of the Boundary Commission got their first real taste of an Indian scare.

On the fourth day of the trip, while advancing into Cooke's Canyon in pursuit of antelope, Cremony suddenly found himself surrounded by approximately twenty-five savages of the band of Cuchillo Negro (Black Knife). Knowing that the carriage would soon come into sight, Cremony drew his revolver and waited. When Cuchillo Negro got within twenty-five yards, Cremony informed him that the warriors might kill him but that he would shoot the chief before dying. Cuchillo Negro then asked what Cremony wanted. The American replied that he and the many who would shortly follow were merely passing through the country and that they came in peace. The Indians did not believe that more Americans were following close behind Cremony, but agreed to wait and see before ordering an attack. Within fifteen minutes the carriage did round a point of the mountain and rumble forward, accompanied by troops that had caught up with it, whereupon Cuchillo Negro advanced toward Cremony holding up his hand and saying, *"Jeunie, jeunie!"* (Friend, friend!). He then turned and rode off.[19]

[18] Cremony, *Life Among the Apaches*, 23.
[19] *Ibid.*, 24-30.

Once in camp at Santa Rita del Cobre, the Americans were visited by more Apaches, members of the bands of Mangas Coloradas, Ponce, and Delgadito. These savages took advantage in subsequent days of Bartlett's trust to drive off the Commission's livestock and to steal everything not heavily guarded. On one occasion Colonel Craig's dragoons had to pursue the Indians on foot — needless to say, fruitlessly — because the savages had stolen the army's horses and mules. Yet Cremony records that during the several months in camp at Santa Rita, Commissioner Bartlett persisted despite all evidence to the contrary in his theory that "kind treatment, a rigid adherence to what is right, and a prompt and invariable fulfillment of all promises, would secure the friendship of the Apaches."

Finally came an incident that proved the perfidy of the Apaches. A band of savages raided a mining camp about three or four miles down the canyon from the Commission's headquarters, stealing a herd of cattle and driving them off. Lieutenant Whipple led approximately twenty members of the Commission in mounted pursuit and came upon the Indians in a wooded area. The Apaches divided into two parties, one to slow the pursuers, the other to hurry the cattle on. A lively fight developed between the savages and Whipple's party, during which Delgadito, the leader of the raiding party, began taunting the Americans by exhibiting his posterior and slapping it — a favorite act of ridicule among Apaches for those they considered inferior warriors. Delgadito did not know that the Boundary Commission had been furnished with a recently perfected weapon, the Wesson rifle, which could shoot with high accuracy for approximately four hundred yards, at that time a remarkable distance — in fact, just about the distance that Delgadito stood from Whipple's party. Cremony, who had one of the new rifles

Valley of the Copper Mines, from the South

— From Emory, Report, *Part I, page 90.*

which he had fitted with special sights, handed his weapon to Wells, Bartlett's carriage driver and a crack shot, and pointed at the cavorting Delgadito. Wells took careful aim and fired at the exposed target, hitting the "seat of honor" squarely and causing "an unearthly yell and a series of dances and capers that would put a *maitre de ballet* to blush," according to Cremony's description. The Indians thereupon fled. The Americans pursued them for thirty miles and came upon the abandoned cattle.[20] Despite this episode Bartlett still clung to his "noble savage" concept.

Once the survey was underway from the Santa Rita encampment, Bartlett indulged himself in a trip southward in May and June of 1851 to Fronteras and other Sonoran towns, most of which he found deserted because of Indian raids. He penetrated as far south as Arizpe, Sonora, before returning to Santa Rita.[21] Shortly after his return came an incident which revealed the Commissioner's romantic and chivalrous attitude toward his duties. On June 27 a party of New Mexican traders, who profited by bartering illicit items to the Apaches for booty and slaves captured in Mexico, rode into the American camp to secure provisions. Cremony discovered in their midst a young Mexican girl, Inez Gonzales; he immediately informed Bartlett of this, and the Commissioner had the dragoons forceably remove her to his tent. He found her "quite young, artless, and interesting in appearance, prepossessing in manners, and by her deportment gave evidence that she had been carefully brought up."[22] The girl later was restored to her parents, married a Mexican captain, and lived to a ripe old age.[23]

[20]*Ibid.,* 82-85; Bartlett, *Personal Narrative,* I, 346-353.

[21]Bartlett to Stuart, Santa Rita del Cobre, July 1, 1851, *SED* 119, pp. 411-416.

[22]Bartlett, *Personal Narrative,* I, 306.

[23]*Ibid.,* I, 303-318; Cremony, *Life Among the Apaches,* 52-57. Bartlett also rescued two captive Mexican lads by force from the Apaches and restored them to their families. See letters in *SED* 119, 258-261.

Just at this juncture the American Surveyor, A. B. Gray, put in his long-delayed appearance, arriving at El Paso on June 24 in company with Lieutenant Colonel James D. Graham, the replacement for Colonel McClellan as chief astronomer with the Boundary Commission. Graham remained in El Paso, but Gray presented himself at the Santa Rita camp on July 19. At a meeting of the Joint Commission held the next day, Gray was asked to examine the proceedings which had been conducted in his absence, and to affix his signature to them. After spending several days going over these papers, Gray declared flatly that the Bartlett-Conde agreement line was "too far north" and gave Mexico "a large and important district of country which was added to the United States by the Treaty of Guadalupe Hidalgo."[24]

In a formal communication to Bartlett on July 25, Gray outlined his reasons for refusing to ratify the initial point agreed upon. He stated first that the Treaty gave full powers to the Commissioners *and* the Surveyors. Second, he reminded Bartlett that when the Joint Commission had adjourned at San Diego, it had agreed that should one party arrive at El Paso before the other, the first one there "could push on its operations as far as practicable, 'subject, of course, to the examination and revision of the other party.'" The Rio Grande could safely have been surveyed during his absence, Gray contended; there was no pressing urgency to settle the initial point on the Rio Grande when so much remained that could have safely been surveyed in his absence. Third, Gray rejected Conde's argument for 32° 22′ by insisting that the true point of reference was the correct latitude of El Paso, "an actual place existing upon the map and

[24]"Report of A. B. Gray, with a map in relation to the Mexican boundary," *SED* 55, 33 Cong., 2 Sess., 4. Hereafter cited as Gray, *Report*.

upon the ground, and likewise mentioned in the treaty." If El Paso had been used as the point of reference, the initial point of the southern boundary of New Mexico would have been placed eight miles north of the town, or 31° 52′ north latitude. Gray stated that El Paso did not appear below the border of New Mexico as Bartlett had put it, but that the border had been placed just north of El Paso deliberately. And he reminded the American Commissioner that Disturnell, in his map of 1849, again placed the town just south of the boundary. The treaty-makers had "scrupulously avoided" the use of parallels and meridians, Gray said, since they wisely preferred "natural objects upon the earth's surface to those imaginary and unmarked lines." The result was that the Treaty drew a "clear and unmistakable description of the boundary from the Pacific to the Gulf of Mexico." The compromise effected by Conde and Bartlett, Gray said in conclusion, used as the initial point a parallel not marked on Disturnell's map and not mentioned in the Treaty. Gray therefore advised "immediate suspension" of the survey along the Bartlett-Conde line, and suggested that the American Commissioner notify the Mexican officials that the "final decision of this line may be changed, from the want of conformation and agreement of your colleague."[25]

Gray was especially vehement in denying both Whipple's right to act as Surveyor *ad interim* and Bartlett's authority to appoint the lieutenant to that office. *"By and with the consent of the Mexican Commissioner,"* Gray indignantly wrote, Bartlett

[25]Gray to Bartlett, Santa Rita del Cobre, July 25, 1851, *SED* 119, pp. 279-284. Bartlett later asserted that Gray had not made known his objections to the compromise line until September 6 at a meeting of the Joint Boundary Commission held that day. See Bartlett, *Personal Narrative,* I, 376. It would appear that Gray either had a better memory of this event, or he was more careful of his statements than was the Commissioner.

was "CONSTITUTING HIMSELF PRESIDENT and General Conde the Senate of the United States . . . ." He even impugned Bartlett's motives in making the compromise:

> Mr. Bartlett was emphatically instructed that the government would expect him to uphold the just rights of his country, and at the same time, that no advantage of Mexico was to be taken. In both respects he failed, for while he did not uphold the rights of his country, he permitted himself to be deluded into the belief that he had obtained a considerable portion of Mexican territory which had not been ceded by the treaty.[26]

On this latter score Gray was correct. When Gray refused to sign the agreement, Bartlett wrote the Secretary of the Interior a letter of justification for the compromise. He stated that the initial point of 32° 22′ was justified because the use of latitudinal markings from the map was "a course any geographer would have pursued if unbiased by sinister motives." Yet he went on to assert that the Disturnell map was wrong by two degrees of longitude. "Who," he asked, "must lose these two degrees, Mexico or the United States? We throw the loss on Mexico by claiming and obtaining, as I have done, the entire length of the southern boundary of New Mexico, in reality taking from her a considerable portion of Sonora." As for the actual site of El Paso being a point of reference in determining the boundary, Bartlett said that the town was but "incidentally mentioned" in the Treaty. "If the line should fall one mile or one hundred miles *north* of El Paso," it would still "conform to the treaty," he wrote. And he pointed out that the map was incorrect in other particulars, specifically that it showed towns that did not exist upon the ground. The thirty-second parallel actually existed, he said, while El Paso was incorrectly placed. Bartlett summed up his position with what he doubtless felt was irrefutable logic:

[26] Gray, *Report,* 13.

"Shall we measure from the one known to be correct [the thirty-second parallel], or the one known to be erroneous [El Paso]? Unquestionably from the correct one."[27]

Angry at Gray's refusal to endorse the agreement he had made with Conde, and probably jealous of his powers in light of Gray's declaration that the Surveyor had joint authority with the Commissioner, Bartlett wrote Gray for a statement of what the Surveyor thought to be his actual authority. Gray replied by acknowledging that the head of each Commission was the Commissioner; however, he insisted that all maps and papers, to be legal, had to be signed by both the Commissioners and the Surveyors — as stated in the Treaty of Guadalupe Hidalgo.[28] Colonel Graham, the chief astronomer, sided with Gray in this quarrel. Graham pointed out that Bartlett's designation of Whipple as Surveyor *ad interim* had not been made until April 23, 1851, the day before the ceremonies were held at the initial point; Whipple therefore had taken no official part in the discussions which resulted in the compromise. Whipple's role had been confined to locating the initial point on the ground and to signing the document deposited at the monument.[29] General Conde, when notified of Gray's refusal to sign, remarked simply that the initial point had been determined according to Article V of the Treaty and to his own satisfaction, and that the decision could not be reversed.[30] Well indeed he might be satisfied with an agreement so beneficial to Mexico.

At this juncture Gray ceased writing Bartlett and began communicating with the Secretary of the Interior in protest to the

[27] Bartlett to Stuart, Santa Rita del Cobre, August 8, 1851, *SED* 119, p. 146.
[28] Gray to Bartlett, Santa Rita del Cobre, August 9, 1851, *ibid.*, 213-214.
[29] J. D. Graham to Stuart, Santa Rita del Cobre, August 16, 1851, *ibid.*, 243-246.
[30] Bartlett, *Personal Narrative,* I, 376.

Bartlett-Conde compromise. On August 3 the Surveyor stated that no argument for 32° 22′ could be sustained. He said he regarded it a "misfortune" that Bartlett had signed away a "large piece of territory belonging to New Mexico, a portion of which is of splendid character, and most important to the United States," and he informed the Secretary of the Interior that he had just received additional Senate documents which confirmed his contention that the boundary should be placed just north of El Paso. These documents, which he specifically had requested, comprised the correspondence between the Secretary of State and Nicholas P. Trist, the agent for the United States who negotiated the Treaty of Guadalupe Hidalgo. According to Gray, this correspondence showed that the negotiators of 1848 could not agree on a specified parallel of latitude as the boundary between the United States and Mexico because Mexico was afraid of losing El Paso, a town that the United States hoped to acquire. Thus all parallels finally were disregarded by the negotiators and the line north of El Paso, shown as the boundary between Chihuahua and New Mexico, was selected. Gray felt that the United States thus was entitled to the land beween 31° 52′ and 32° 22′ and should have it.[31]

At stake in the controversy over the Bartlett-Conde agreement was a strip of land thirty-five miles wide by 175.28 miles long — more than six thousand square miles of territory. The intensity of the dispute arose from the varying opinions as to the worth of the land and the use to which it could be put. According to Bartlett the only value of the Mesilla strip, as the area came to be called, was the land immediately adjacent to the Rio Grande. This land, which averaged one and a half miles in width, was worth from fifty cents to one dollar an acre in the Commis-

[31]Gray to Stuart, Santa Rita del Cobre, August 3, 1851, *SED* 119, 298-300.

sioner's estimation. "Beyond this west," he wrote, "is a desert without water, wood, or grass, where not *one acre* can ever be cultivated, where no military post can be sustained, and which can never be inhabited." One small village, Mesilla, was in the disputed area, he noted, but it consisted "of mud or chiefly of stick houses," and was inhabited by Mexicans who had abandoned Santa Fe rather than become American citizens. Should this town come under the jurisdiction of the United States, Bartlett asserted that three-fourths of these people would remove themselves south of the new boundary and thus again be under Mexican jurisdiction.[32]

Gray had a sharply different opinion as to the worth of the Mesilla Strip. Prefacing his remarks on this subject with the statement that the value of the land had nothing to do with the the validity of the American claim to it, the Surveyor accused Bartlett of trying to "underrate it and place a low estimate upon its importance . . . ." This valley, Gray declared, was far from worthless, it was "one of the most beautiful and fertile along the course of the Rio Grande." The soil, he stated, was "proverbial for its productivity," and would grow most varieties of fruits and vegetables."[33]

Many times more important than the productivity of the soil, however, was the use to which the area could be put — specifically, as the route of a transcontinental railroad. Article VI of the Treaty of Guadalupe Hidalgo referred to the possibility of constructing a road, canal, or railway through the country along the Gila River. The United States needed such a link with the Pacific Coast, and thus was vitally interested in any strip of land which had the potential of a passageway to the newly acquired

[32]Bartlett to Stuart, Santa Rita del Cobre, August 8, 1851, *ibid.,* 145-149.
[33]Gray, *Report,* 27-28.

West Coast. Bartlett stated that a practicable railroad route could be found entirely north of 32° 22′. Once again Gray differed with the Commissioner, pointing out that in the disputed area was a natural break in the Rocky Mountains which was "free from heavy snows" and had "uninterrupted communications the whole year round." On such a route free of steep grades, a railroad could be built with little effort. The Mesilla Valley should not be surrendered, argued Gray, since it commanded "the great gateway to the Pacific."[34] In his opinion any railroad built across the southern United States would have to be "from the region of El Paso, over the disputed district to the Gila, and down the valley of that stream to the Colorado," and thence to San Diego.[35]

What Gray did not know when he was busily dispatching letters to Washington was that both the Secretary of the Interior and the Secretary of War had agreed to the boundary as set by Bartlett and Conde. There is a definite probability that Secretary Stuart, in supporting Bartlett was consciously defending a political appointee of the Whig administration. The following year would bring another national election, and the Whigs, then enjoying what would prove to be their last national administration, were fearful of defeat. Another probable cause of their concurrence with Bartlett's interpretation was that available information indicated that the land below 32° 22′ was worth-

[34] *Ibid.*, 28-33.

[35] *Ibid.* That others agreed with the Surveyor is shown by the Robert Mills' memorial. The map accompanying this report traced the proposed route for a transcontinental railroad. The track was to run from El Paso to the Rio Gila through the disputed area, and then on to San Diego. See "Map of the Country Between the Atlantic and Pacific Oceans, included within the latitudes 25 and 42 and the longitudes 75 & 123 West, shewing [*sic*] the proposed route of a Rail Road from the Mississippi Valley to the ports of San Diego, Monterey & San Francisco . . .," *Senate Report* C44, 32 Cong., 1 Sess., 18.

less — and therefore fit only for Indians, who in that vicinity were troublesome, and who were the responsibility of the United States.

Since the first Spanish settlements had been established in northern New Spain, the Apaches and Comanches had raided and looted to secure their livelihood. These nomadic savages lived by the chase, securing status by theft and murder. Their raids had been reduced during the last years of Spanish rule by means of the *establecimientos de paz* (establishments of peace) where the Indians were settled and periodically given presents — *i.e.,* peace was bought by giving the Indians more than they could steal.[36] After the Mexican Revolution had succeeded, the presents and rations had ceased and the Apaches and Comanches had thundered out of the period of peace with ever-increasing frequency. Life and property became unsafe in northern Mexico because of this bloody scourge, and because of the political instability of that republic no solution had been found.[37] Then in 1848 came the Treaty of Guadalupe Hidalgo, an instrument which the Mexicans used to transfer the problem to the United States. Article XI of the Treaty stated:

Considering that a great part of the territories which, by the present Treaty, are to be comprehended for the future within the limits of the United States, is now occupied by savage tribes, who will hereafter be under the exclusive control of the Government of the United States, and whose incursions within the territory of Mexico would be prejudicial in the extreme; it is solemnly agreed that all such incursions shall be forcibly restrained by the Government of the United States, whensoever this

[36]For a study of Spanish-Indian relations in the Southwest, see Sidney B. Brinckerhoff and Odie B. Faulk, *Lancers for the King* (Phoenix: Arizona Historical Foundation, 1965), 81-92.

[37]For this story see Ralph A. Smith, "Indians in American-Mexican Relations Before the War of 1846," *Hispanic American Historical Review,* XLIII (February 1963), 34-64; Robert C. Stevens, "The Apache Menace in Sonora, 1831-1849," *Arizona and the West,* VI (Autumn 1964), 211-222.

> may be necessary; and that when they cannot be prevented, they shall be punished by the said Government, and satisfaction for the same shall be exacted; all in the same way, and with equal diligence and energy, as if the same incursions were meditated or committed within its own territory against its own citizens.[38]

The United States had not found this new duty easily performed.[39] In fact, by the summer of 1851 they had found restraining the Comanches and Apaches almost impossible, either against Americans or Mexicans. James S. Calhoun, a Georgian appointed the first Indian Agent in New Mexico following the conquest, wrote Commissioner of Indian Affairs William Medill on July 22, 1849: "The gravest subject with our Indian affairs in New Mexico relates to the wandering tribes, who have never cultivated the soil, and have supported themselves by depredations alone. This is the only labor known to them." In this same letter Calhoun summed up admirably the crux of the Indian problem in the Southwest: "The thought of annihilating these Indians cannot be entertained by an American public — nor can the Indians abandon their predatory incursions, and live and learn to support themselves by the sweat of their own brows . . . ."[40] Less than a month later, on August 16, Calhoun again wrote the Commissioner: "The Indians generally, are in a bad temper. The number of troops are not sufficient to keep upon them a proper check . . . ."[41]

[39]For the full story of the attempt to control the Apaches following the Mexican War, see Ralph H. Ogle, "Federal Control of the Western Apaches," *New Mexico Historical Review,* XIV and XV (October 1939 and January 1940),

[38]Malloy, *Treaties,* 1110.

309-365 and 12-71.

[40]James S. Calhoun to William Medill, Santa Fe, July 22, 1849, "Report of the Commissioner of Indian Affairs, 1850," quoted in William A. Keleher, *Turmoil in New Mexico, 1846-1869* (Santa Fe: The Rydall Press, 1952), 45. For a biographical sketch of Calhoun, see Calvin Horn, *New Mexico's Troubled Years* (Albuquerque: Horn and Wallace, 1963), 21-35.

[41]Quoted in Keleher, *Turmoil in New Mexico,* 46.

Time and again Calhoun wrote of the deteriorating situation in New Mexico. Finally he summed up what would be needed to control the savages:

To establish a proper state of affairs in this country, with the economy which the government of the United States should and will ever observe, requires a strong arm, and a prompt arm, guided by an enlightened patriotism. Expend your million now, if necessary, that you may avoid the expenditure of millions hereafter . . . . The Comanches and Apaches, with all their fragments of other tribes, must be penned up, and this should be done at the earliest possible day . . . .[42]

Nor had the situation improved by the summer of 1851 when Bartlett and Gray were disagreeing. Colonel Edwin V. Sumner, who assumed command of the Department of New Mexico on July 19, 1851, continually wrote pessimistic reports to Washington about the Indian problem and about the country in general. His report of May 27, 1852, summed up his attitude: "So long as we hold this country, as we do now, it must be a very heavy burden to us; and there never can be the slightest return for all this outlay . . . . Twenty — fifty years hence — this Territory will be precisely the same it is now. There can never be any inducement for any class of our people to come here whose example will improve this people." Concerning the Indians he wrote, "If the Mexicans should act justly by the Indians, I think there would be no difficulty; but if they did not, and war should ensue, the Mexicans would always steal from the Indians quite as much as the Indians would steal from them, and thus there would be no losers in the end."[43]

[42]Quoted in *ibid.*, 54.

[43]Edwin V. Sumner, "Reports from the Ninth Military Department, New Mexico," Santa Fe, May 27, 1852, *SED* 1, 32 Cong., 2 Sess., Part II, 25.

The situation was so deplorable that by 1852 the Secretary of War, Charles Magill Conrad (who served in that office from August 15, 1850, to March 7, 1853) declared:

Would it not be better to induce the inhabitants [of New Mexico] to abandon a country which seems hardly fit for the habitation of civilized man, by remunerating them for their property in money or lands situated in more favorable regions? Even if the government paid for the property quintuple its value, it would still, merely on the score of economy, be largely the gainer by the transaction, and the troops now stationed in New Mexico would be available for the protection of other portions of our own and of the Mexican territory. Unless the means I have indicated, or some others, be adopted to relieve the Indians from the necessity of plundering to procure the means of subsistence, their depredations must not only continue, but increase. This would require a corresponding increase in the means of protection.[44]

Mexico was assuming the position that it was the responsibility of the American government to pay for all damages inflicted by the Indians living north of the border and raiding below it.[45] Many claims had been filed by Mexican victims of Apache and Comanche incursions, claims that were bought at a discount by speculators in Mexico City; these speculators in turn were bringing pressure to bear on their government to get payment, and hence a demand on this score in Washington. In the War and State departments, therefore, it was felt that the "worthless" strip of territory which Bartlett had signed away would reduce somewhat the number of Indians living on the American side of the border. Give it back to Mexico was the prevailing thought in Washington — give it back and thus re-

[44]"Report of the Secretary of War," *ibid.,* 6.

[45]For the Mexican attitude about these Indian raids, see Manuel Robles, *Memoria del Secretario de Estado y del Despacho de Guerro y Marina* (Mexico City: Vicente G. Torres, 1852), 48.

duce the extent of the problem, as well as protect a political appointee.

Secretary Stuart was exceedingly vexed when notified that Gray had refused to sign the Bartlett-Conde compromise. In connection with the Surveyor's contention that both Commissioner and Surveyor had to sign all documents to make them legal, Stuart wrote Gray that he was "not aware" that the Surveyor had "ever claimed any right to participate in the deliberations" of the Joint Commission, "much less to exercise a supervisory power."[46] He reasoned that since the Commissioners had compromised and were satisfied with the initial point, it was "desirable" that all papers necessary to settling the matter be "perfected." He therefore "requested" Gray to "remove the only obstacle which now exists to the completion of this branch of the work, by affixing your signature to the requisite papers."[47] This order was dated October 31, 1851. Four days later, long before it could have reached Gray, the Secretary fired Gray from the Boundary Commission.[48]

In the midst of this conflict of opinion with Gray, Bartlett had become embroiled in a jurisdictional quarrel with Lieutenant Colonel James D. Graham, the topographical engineer named to replace McClellan. Graham, born in 1799 in Virginia, had graduated from West Point in 1817, and had been commissioned a second lieutenant in the artillery. From 1819 to 1821 he served

[46]"Report of the Committee on Foreign Relations . . . in relation to fixing the initial point in the boundary line between the United States and Mexico . . . August 20, 1852," *Senate Report* 345, 32 Cong., 1 Sess., 5. In his *Report*, Gray pointed out that Stuart had written him while at San Diego on October 8, 1850, that "the 5th article of the treaty of Guadalupe Hidalgo requires the . . . presence of such *surveyor*" to fulfill its stipulation. Gray, *Report,* 17.

[47]Stuart to Gray, Washington, October 31, 1851, *SED* 119, 118.

[48]"Report on fixing the initial point . . .," *Senate Report* 345, 32 Cong., 1 Sess., 4.

as first assistant to Major Stephen H. Long on Long's expedition to the Rocky Mountains, a task that greatly interested him in topographical engineering and which shaped his subsequent career. When the Topographical Engineers was created a separate corps in 1838, Graham was commissioned a major in it. He was the astronomer on the American Commission that surveyed the boundary between the United States and Texas in 1839—the same commission on which Gray had served for the Lone Star Republic. He then had helped survey the boundary between Maine and Canada, for which he was breveted a lieutenant colonel. Following this, he had directed the resurvey of the Mason-Dixon Line. Then in 1850, following the removal of McClellan from the Boundary Commission, Graham was appointed "principal astronomer and chief of the scientific corps."[49]

Bartlett and Graham almost instantly took a dislike to one another, even before they met in person. Graham arrived at El Paso in company with Surveyor A. B. Gray, and the following day addressed a note to Bartlett to that effect. Inadvertently, however, Graham's clerk sent the penciled copy of this letter, which constituted in those days a grave insult.[50] Heated letters followed between the two, the upshot of which was that Bartlett refused to recognize Graham as head of the "Scientific Corps." The Commissioner insisted that the word "Topographical" had been omitted in the colonel's letter of appointment and should have preceded "Scientific Corps," thus considerably reducing Graham's authority. Graham was a proud and strong-willed professional soldier, determined to uphold what he considered to be the authority vested in himself by his appointment. Bartlett, on the other hand, was jealous of any real or fancied en-

[49]Stuart to Bartlett, Washington, October 23, 1850, *SED* 121, 72.
[50]Graham to Bartlett, Frontera, June 26, 1851, *ibid.*, 129.

croachment upon his right to be the uncontested head of the entire Commission. Two such individuals were bound to quarrel.

This unfortunate affair reached a climax shortly after Graham's arrival. The same day he notified Bartlett of his arrival, the colonel ordered Lieutenant Whipple, then engaged in the survey of the southern boundary of New Mexico, to report to him at El Paso. Three days later Graham ordered all work on the southern boundary of New Mexico suspended until he could inspect it as "head of the scientific corps, appointed by the President of the United States," and he informed all members of the "Scientific Corps" to submit to him a full list of all instruments in their possession.[51]

Bartlett responded to these orders with a roar of indignation, especially after Graham ordered a halt to the survey of the southern boundary of New Mexico. Graham further angered the Commissioner by agreeing with Gray that the Bartlett-Conde agreement deprived the United States of territory rightfully belonging to it. Bartlett's mode of reprisal to these differences was a refusal to recognize Graham as "head of the scientific corps." Graham responded by ordering the quartermaster, an army officer, to issue no "provisions or property, unless on requisitions communicated through me, with my approval attached thereto." Graham took several other steps to force Bartlett to recognize him as head of the scientific corps. The new commissary and quartermaster of the Boundary Commission, Lieutenant Ambrose E. Burnside,[52] had arrived at El Paso in company

[51]Graham to Whipple, Frontera, June 26 and 29, 1851, and Graham, "Circular," Frontera, June 29, 1851, *SED,* 130, 137, 138.

[52]Ambrose Everett Burnside a native of Indiana and a graduate of West Point (class of 1843), later would become a major general of volunteers during the Civil War, then senator from and governor of Rhode Island. He gained enduring fame for his type of side-whiskers, which to this day bear his name.

Town of El Paso on the Rio Grande

— *By Charles Shuchard, from* The A. B. Gray Report.

with Graham, and he knew how to play the "Army game." Knowing which side in the dispute would be to his long-run advantage, Burnside sided with Graham, as did Lieutenant Whipple. Burnside did not stay long with the Commission, however; he was soon dispatched to Washington with personal letters from Graham to Colonel John J. Abert, the commander of the Corps of Topographical Engineers.

Both Graham and Bartlett began sending long letters to Secretary Stuart explaining their sides of the controversy. Each seemed confident that he would be upheld and his adversary reprimanded. Stuart again sided with Bartlett. The Secretary of the Interior wrote the Secretary of War that Colonel Graham had misinterpreted his instructions, that he had been extremely slow to join the Commission in the field, and that his refusal to issue instruments had caused delays which General Conde had protested. Stuart asked that Graham be recalled and Major Emory be reappointed as chief astronomer.[53]

The details of the quarrel between Graham and Bartlett arrived in Washington just when Secretary Stuart was being vexed by Gray's refusal to sign the Bartlett-Conde agreement. Stuart, after writing the letter of October 31, 1851, ordered Gray to sign, decided to combine the offices of surveyor and chief astronomer — both tasks being assigned to Major Emory. The Secretary justified this dual appointment by saying it was done "in order to reduce as much as possible the expenses of the Mexican boundary commission, and with a view to the harmonious, correct, and expeditious prosecutions of the survey . . . ." Emory was given a copy of the order which Stuart had sent

[53]For details of this controversy, see various letters in *SED* 121, 138-147; and Stuart to the Secretary of War, Washington, September 11, 1851, *SED* 119, 113-114.

Gray with instructions that, if Gray had persisted in his refusal to sign the Bartlett-Conde agreement, he was to do so.[54] Emory despite his dislike of duty with this Commission had no recourse but to obey his orders; thus he again found himself attached to the United States-Mexican boundary survey.

These changes ordered by the Secretary of the Interior would take time to reach the Commission in New Mexico, however. Because of Graham's refusal to issue instruments for a survey of the southern boundary of New Mexico, Bartlett was forced to modify his program of surveying.

[54] "Report on fixing the initial point . . .," *Senate Report* 345, 32 Cong., 1 Sess., 4; Stuart to Emory, Washington, November 4, 1851, *SED* 119, 121.

VI

SURVEYING THE GILA AND RIO GRANDE

BECAUSE OF A. B. Gray and Graham, the survey along the Bartlett-Conde compromise line was halted late in July of 1851. The Commissioners thereupon decided to leave one party at El Paso del Norte to commence working down the Rio Grande, and to assign the remainder to work on the Gila River. Colonel Graham was detailed to head the party surveying the Texas-Mexican river boundary; Gray and Whipple were to undertake the work on the Gila. These two rivers, Bartlett had concluded, could safely be run and marked while the Joint Commission was awaiting a decision on the southern boundary of New Mexico from Washington and Mexico City. Owing to an oversight, however, most of the supplies of the American party had been left at El Paso and thus were unavailable to Gray and Whipple. Bartlett decided at that point that he would set himself the task of procuring more supplies in Sonora — which would necessitate another trip through the countryside and which would make the book he was writing about his experiences in the Southwest that much more interesting.

With fifty-four men, including Gray and Whipple, the American Commissioner left Santa Rita del Cobre on August 27 with only a fifteen-day supply of food. Their destination was the Gila River where a rendezvous had been scheduled with General Conde and a Mexican surveying party; Conde had previously taken part of his Commission westward, sending the remainder to El Paso under Surveyor Salazar to work on the survey of the Rio Grande. Colonel Graham, instead of returning to El Paso as he had been ordered, insisted on accompanying the American party westward in order, as he put it, to acquaint General Conde with his side of the dispute between himself and Bartlett. The two parties met on September 6 approximately twenty miles east of the San Pedro River, and a meeting of the Joint Boundary Commission was held. Conde listened to Graham politely but made no comment on the quarrel, announcing instead that he planned a trip to the Sonoran town of Santa Cruz to obtain supplies. Gray and Whipple thereupon departed to begin their work on the Gila, while Bartlett chose to accompany Conde southward. Graham went along with the two Commissioners to the town of Santa Cruz. No supplies were to be had there, but Graham evidently found the scenery pleasant for Bartlett subsequently complained in a letter to the Secretary of the Interior that the colonel was still at Santa Cruz thirty-one days after leaving the copper mines at Santa Rita and seventeen days after his interview with General Conde.[1]

From Santa Cruz Bartlett sent word to Gray to continue the survey of the Gila. The American Commissioner said he had decided to journey farther south into Sonora in search of supplies, and would rejoin the party on that river as soon as pos-

[1]Bartlett to Stuart, Santa Cruz, Sonora, September 27, 1851, *SED* 119, 456-462.

sible.[2] Bartlett went from Santa Cruz to Ures, arriving there on October 13. Shortly thereafter he fell ill with some type of fever and was extremely sick for a time. A month later he wrote Secretary Stuart that he was better but had not completely recovered.[3] He remained at Ures another month and a half recuperating, then left on December 29 for Hermosillo, where he arrived on New Year's Day of 1852.[4] There he arrived at the conclusion that the easiest way to rejoin Gray and Whipple on the Gila was to go by boat to San Diego and then overland to Fort Yuma. Therefore he proceeded to the port of Mazatlan. At that city he received the news that General Conde had died at Arizpe, Sonora, on December 19, the victim of typhus. Bartlett was saddened, he wrote, for he thought Conde an "amiable and estimable gentleman."[5]

From Mazatlan Bartlett took a coastal steamer southward to Acapulco, leaving behind ten of his party to make their way overland to rejoin the surveying party on the Gila. At Acapulco on February 1, Bartlett boarded the *Oregon,* a vessel already overcrowded with 472 immigrants bound for California. He had to use his rank as "a government officer charged with important duties" to get aboard the ship. After an uneventful voyage of eight days, the *Oregon* arrived at San Diego on February 9.[6] The Commissioner had been absent from his duties on the survey for five months, had traveled more than two thousand miles, yet had acomplished nothing of value to the United States.

[2]Gray to Bartlett, Santa Cruz, Sonora, September 24, 1851, *ibid.,* 267-269.
[3]Bartlett to Stuart, Ures, Sonora, November 12, 1851, *ibid.,* 463.
[4]Bartlett to Stuart, Hermosillo, Sonora, January 1, 1852, *ibid.,* 150.
[5]Bartlett, *Personal Narrative,* I, 455-456.
[6]*Ibid.,* 503-505; Bartlett to Stuart, Mazatlan, Mexico, January 10, 1852, *SED* 119, 464; Bartlett to Stuart, San Diego, February 16, 1852, *ibid.,* 465.

The party left behind by Bartlett included his friend Dr. Thomas H. Webb, the artist Henry Pratt, and the interpreter John C. Cremony, in all a party of ten men. Having made the long trek westward with Bartlett, they knew the hazards of the country and the fickleness of the savages. All were well armed, except Dr. Webb, who carried nothing but a knife and a small five-inch five-shooter. North they went through Sonora to the Santa Cruz Valley, then down it past Tubac, San Xavier del Bac, and Tucson to the Gila River and the Pima villages, where they turned westward. After several adventures with the Indians, particularly the Yumas, they reached the stretch of desert between present Yuma and their goal of San Diego. Near the old battleground of San Pascual they met American troops under the command of Major Samuel P. Heintzelman on their way to reoccupy Fort Yuma and to punish the Yuma Indians for their many depredations.[7] The ten men finally staggered into San Diego footsore and weary, arriving two days after Bartlett.[8]

While these events had been transpiring, Gray, Whipple, and their party had been carrying on the work of surveying the boundary and having their share of adventures. Following their

[7]What would become Fort Yuma was first established at the site of the old Spanish mission of Puerto de la Concepción by Lieutenant Cave J. Couts and his troops of the 1st Dragoons on October 2, 1849. The post was named Camp Calhoun in honor of the great Senator from South Carolina, John C. Calhoun, former Secretary of War and Secretary of State. It remained there until December 1, 1850, when it was moved by Major Samuel P. Heintzelman to a point just below the ferry crossing, at which time it was designated Camp Independence. The post was abandoned in March of 1851, then reestablished on the site of Camp Calhoun and renamed Camp Yuma after the Indians in that vicinity. Its primary purpose in those early days was to keep an eye on the Yumas and to assist emigrant parties of gold seekers bound for the digs in California. See Ray Brandes, *Frontier Military Posts of Arizona* (Globe, Arizona: Dale Stuart King, 1960), 81-86. For a history of American-Yuman relations, as well as a history of the Yuma Indians, see Jack D. Forbes, *Warriors of the Colorado* (Norman: University of Oklahoma Press, 1965).

[8]Cremony, *Life Among the Apaches,* 89-128.

orders, they had begun work on October 10 just below the San Carlos branch of the Gila. By December 24 they had run and marked the boundary westward for some 350 miles — *i.e.,* to within sixty miles of the junction of the Gila and the Colorado. This work was done, as Gray later wrote his superiors in Washington, with no guide, few supplies, and only a small military escort of twenty-five men under Lieutenant Colonel Craig. They had to halt the survey because Gray had no more money with which to pay his workers, their supplies were dangerously low, and they had heard nothing from Bartlett. Gray bragged in his report, with considerable justification, that this survey of the Gila constituted "*more than double* the whole of the work heretofore done, and as dangerous and difficult, if not more so, than any other portion of the whole boundary," and at "one-tenth of the *entire expenditures* in the field."[9]

Carefully marking the spot where they terminated the survey of the Gila, Gray and Whipple took their men westward to the junction of the Gila and Colorado where a military post was thought to exist, but which in fact had been abandoned.[10] Instead of a troop of American soldiers, the weary party was met by "an array of 1500 Indians, the flower of the Yuma nation." The Indians were in possession of the two flatboats used as the ferry, and the river was then a quarter of a mile wide and from fifteen to thirty feet deep. The Americans were informed that they could not cross, and therefore went into camp for the night expecting to be attacked before dawn. During the night the interpreter with the party learned that the Yumas planned to massacre the Americans; therefore they made a breastwork of

[9]Gray to Stuart, San Diego, January 10, 1852, *SED* 119, 305-307.

[10]Abandoned late in December of 1851, the post was not re-garrisoned until February 22, 1852. See above, note 7.

their wagons and property. The day passed with no attack, the preparations of the Americans apparently causing the Indians to pause and think.

Toward nightfall Chief Azul and his leading warrior known as Juan Antonio approached the camp. He wanted to know how much money the Americans had with them and where it was kept. Whipple informed the chief that he would be paid two dollars apiece to ferry the men across the river and one dollar for each horse and mule. During the course of the interview, the families of the two chiefs wandered into the American camp, apparently curious about the visitors. Suddenly a young Indian girl, about fourteen or fifteen years old, moved forward and whispered in the ear of her father, Juan Antonio; he in turn called Chief Azul aside and whispered to him. Other Indians wandered up and joined the mysterious conference, and as soon as they whispered for a while every savage eye was turned on Lieutenant Whipple. Finally the interpreter spoke to the lieutenant: "These warriors think they have seen you before. They would like to know whether you came to the Colorado river from San Diego, on the Pacific coast, two years ago, and camped on the hill opposite this present camp?"

Whipple replied affirmatively, whereupon the young Indian maid arose and came forward with her father. "I saw by the expression of delight on the face of the interpreters," later wrote Frank Wheaton, "that all danger was past." The reason for the Indians' change of intentions soon became clear. Two years previously when Whipple was at the junction of the Gila and Colorado rivers making observations, he had found the Indian girl in a state of hunger and suffering. He had taken her to his tent where he had given her a watermelon and, as a present, a small mirror. She had not forgotten the favor, and within an hour the Yumas were busy ferrying the party across the river.[11]

Gray, Whipple, and their men reached San Diego on January 8, 1852. Two days later Gray wrote Secretary of the Interior Stuart for instructions and for information about Commissioner Bartlett.[12] Almost a month later, Bartlett arrived by sea from Acapulco and the Boundary Commission was reunited. However, everyone was not happy. In fact, many of the men were sick of wandering in the desert with few supplies and infrequent pay. Bartlett therefore paid off a high percentage of the Commission's civilian employees, who immediately rushed northward to the gold fields. The troops of Colonel Craig's military escort likewise became infected with gold fever, and several of them deserted.

Once the Commission was slimmed down to a dedicated few, Bartlett turned his attention to the problem of getting back on the job of surveying. The animals were in poor condition for a trek back across the desert to El Paso, and supplies were almost non-existent. The Commissioner therefore decided it would be necessary to procure more of both — and that to do the job he would have to go northward to San Francisco. The end of February found him in San Francisco, and soon he was journeying about the countryside — Benecia Barracks, the Napa Valley, the redwood forests, San Jose, New Almaden quicksilver mine, and Monterey. He even visited the famous Sutter's Fort. In April he sailed from San Francisco for San Diego; he had not procured sufficient supplies and animals for the Boundary Commission, but he had enjoyed a very nice tour of northern California.

[11]"The Boundary Line: Trials and Adventures of the Surveyors as Described by General Frank Wheaton," Tucson *Arizona Daily Citizen,* July 27, 1895.

[12]Gray to Stuart, San Diego, January 10, 1852, *SED* 119, 305-307.

Upon reaching San Diego, the Commissioner received a packet of correspondence from Washington — dispatches which informed him that both Gray and Colonel Graham had been removed and that Major Emory had been appointed both Surveyor and chief astronomer with orders to proceed to El Paso. Gray and his men immediately were paid off and discharged. And at this point John C. Cremony, the interpreter, resigned. Cremony likewise had received letters from Washington — letters that indicated the Boundary Commission had an uncertain future at least under the leadership of John Bartlett.[13] To replace Cremony, the Commissioner hired Antoine Leroux, one of the great guides of the Southwest, but also one of the most unsung. Leroux was born in St. Louis apparently near the turn of the nineteenth century. He had gone down the Santa Fe Trail to Taos in 1822, where he married and received a Mexican land grant. He was with the James Ohio Pattie fur trapping expedition into Arizona in 1826-1827, had guided Philip St. George Cooke and the Mormon Battalion from Santa Fe to San Diego in 1846-1847, and had held the same position with the surveying party headed by Captain Lorenzo Sitgreaves which surveyed the Zuñi and Little Colorado rivers in 1851 and 1852. The Sitgreaves expedition had disbanded in San Diego, and thus Leroux was in that city without employment in the spring of 1852 when Bartlett began looking for a guide.[14]

At San Diego Bartlett completed his provisioning, but not before pausing to visit the historic missions of San Luis Rey and San Diego. While at the southern port city of San Diego, the Commissioner was entertained by the local commander of troops,

[13]Cremony, *Life Among the Apaches,* 129-130.

[14]For a detailed study of this undeservedly obscure figure, see Forbes Parkhill, *The Blazed Trail of Antoine Leroux* (Los Angeles: Westernlore Press, 1965).

Colonel John Bankhead Magruder — known far and wide as "Prince John" because of the lavishness of his hospitality. Later Magruder would prove to be one of the most dashing of the Confederate generals. But at last Bartlett had to leave the haunts of civilization — and of creature comforts — and push eastward to El Paso. The members of the Boundary Commission left San Diego on May 31, 1852. At that time there were fifty men, including the military escort, in the party. Colonel Craig's twenty-five men of the 3rd Infantry had been reduced to five by desertion for the gold fields, but Magruder loaned Craig ten troops to see the Commission across to El Paso, making a total of fifteen soldiers to protect the thirty-five civilians.[15]

The first portion of the trek eastward, the crossing to Fort Yuma, was marred by tragedy and made uncomfortable by terrible heat. Bartlett wrote one of his San Francisco acquaintances of this march:

> The country is a dreadful one to cross — unquestionably the worst between the Atlantic and Pacific oceans. The entire distance . . . consists of hills, mountains and a desert of 125 miles. The hills are long, steep, sideling [sloping] and rocky. Two wagons were upset and one abandoned — my little wagon bought in San Francisco came in with a broken axle tree and other injuries, and I may say we were all pretty well used up. It was so hot during the day that we were compelled to remain in camp and make our journies [*sic*] at night, starting at sunset. On the desert the thermometer stood in the sun, to which it was exposed, at 140° and in the tents and the most shady places we could find, at from 104 to 114 degrees. Water was only found at great distances apart in wells recently dug, and then but very poor and muddy. But with these little privations we reached the place in good health.[16]

[15]For the story of Bartlett's California interlude, see Bartlett, *Personal Narrative,* II, 1-111.

[16]Bartlett to J. B. Moore, Camp Yuma, Colorado River, June 11, 1852 (MSS in Holliday Collection, Arizona Pioneers' Historical Society, Tucson).

The Rio Grande, near Frontera

— *From Emory,* Report, *Part I, page 46.*

It was during this crossing that Colonel Craig was murdered. On June 5 at Sackett's Well[17] Lieutenant Thomas W. Sweeny, who was stationed at Fort Yuma, rode in with news that he was searching for two deserters from Major Heintzelman's command at the post on the Colorado River. Sweeny said he believed he had passed by the two deserters, and that the Commission thus was likely to meet them as they traveled toward Fort Yuma. The next day, June 6, Bartlett rode ahead of the rest of his group and encamped for the day. As Craig and the remainder of the column moved forward, they met two men on the road. From the dress and muskets of the strangers, Colonel Craig immediately recognized them as the deserters Sweeny was hunting. Bartlett described to Postmaster Jacob B. Moore of San Francisco the events that followed — facts which he ascertained from eyewitnesses:

> [Craig] accused them and tried to prevail on them to surrender to him and return to Camp Yuma. They refused, levelled their guns at him and declared that they would [shoot] the first man who attempted their arrest. The colonel who was a very kind hearted man still believed he could prevail on the men to return without coercive measures. He would not therefore call his soldiers, of which there were eleven, to aid him, but sent for two sergeants to follow him. The deserters then set off on a run, followed by Colonel C — and his two sergeants — the three latter mounted on mules, the deserters on foot. When they came up to the men, the colonel dismounted, threw off his revolver and sabre, and approached within five feet of them, telling them who he was and that he had no intention of using coersive [*sic*] measures. He then told one of his sergeants to stop his [Craig's] mule which was walking off — and as soon as this man was out of the way, one of the deserters said to the other "now is our time, there are but two here" — when they levelled their muskets and fired. The colonel was shot in the lower part of his

[17] This spot was located approximately two and one half miles northwest of the modern Plaster City, which is some seventeen miles west of El Centro. It was named for Russell Sackett, a station keeper.

body and died within ten minutes without speaking — Sargeant [*sic*] Bales[18] was hit by two buck shot, which passing through his leg, killed his mule. In the affray he discharged the colonel's six shooter at the deserters, but without effect owing to the staggering of his wounded mule. The other Sargeant [*sic*] then approached but was driven off by the fire of the deserters, when he made his way to my camp.[19]

Bartlett immediately ordered Dr. Webb and a party to retrace the thirty miles to the spot of the incident and recover the body of Colonel Craig and discover the whereabouts of Sergeant Bales. The body was recovered about sunrise the next day, and on the return trip they found the wounded sergeant. Craig was buried in the desert, Bartlett reading the funeral service.[20] The two deserters, Private John Condon and Corporal William Hayes, subsequently were captured by Indians and turned over to Colonel Magruder at San Diego. There they were court-martialed, found guilty, and hanged at San Diego.[21]

At Fort Yuma Bartlett paused to enjoy the hospitality of Major Heintzelman and to order Lieutenant Whipple to complete the survey of the remaining sixty miles of the Gila River. The day after their arrival, July 12, the Commissioner received a report that during the night the Yuma Indians had entered his camp and made off with fifteen horses and mules, including the fine Kentucky horse which he had purchased from Gray in San Diego. This theft had been accomplished despite the fact

[18]Lieutenant Sweeny spelled the sergeant's name "Beales." See Arthur Woodward (ed.), *Journal of Lt. Thomas W. Sweeny, 1849-1853* (Los Angeles: Westernlore Press, 1956), 163. Bartlett in his *Personal Narrative,* II, 136, spelled it still differently — "Bale."

[19]Bartlett to Moore, Camp Yuma, Colorado River, June 11, 1852. In his version of this affair, Lieutenant Sweeny does not differ from Bartlett's version. See Woodward (ed.), *Journal of Lt. Sweeny,* 159-164.

[20]*Ibid.*; Bartlett, *Personal Narrative,* II, 130-147. Craig's remains later were moved to San Pasqual for decent burial, and still later permanently interred on Point Loma near San Diego. Fort Craig, New Mexico, was named for him.

[21]Woodward (ed.), *Journal of Lt. Sweeny,* 161, 254.

that two men had been standing guard. A half-hearted pursuit was made, but none of the animals were recovered. Leroux said the Yumas could be caught, but only by pursuing them relentlessly for several days. Bartlett did not have the time — he already had been absent from the survey for nearly a year, and thus pushed on toward El Paso without the animals.

While Whipple completed the sixty-mile survey of the unfinished portion of the Gila, Bartlett visited with the Coco-Maricopa Indians and enjoyed their hospitality. He also stopped at the Casa Grande ruins near present Phoenix, Arizona. He found three buildings still standing; these he carefully sketched, drew their floor plans, and copied every hieroglyphic he found. "After three hours spent at the ruins, the hottest, I think, I ever experienced," he later wrote, "we set out on our return to camp."[22] The survey of the Gila completed, Bartlett started in earnest for El Paso. The trip was made from Casa Grande by way of Cooke's Wagon Road to Tucson, San Xavier del Bac, Tubac, and Janos, Chihuahua. After a very hot journey of eighty-one days, the group arrived safely at the Pass of the North on August 17 — almost a year to the day since they began their westward trek from Santa Rita del Cobre. There he learned that Major Emory no longer was in the vicinity but was busy surveying the lower part of the Rio Grande.

Emory indeed had been busy since his appointment as Surveyor and chief astronomer of the Boundary Commission. He had arrived at El Paso on November 25, 1851, where he relieved Colonel Graham. He found the situation chaotic. Approximately one hundred employees of the American Commission were idle for lack of work. Emory reported to the Secretary of the Interior that Bartlett was absent, and no one had definite knowledge of

[22]Bartlett, *Personal Narrative,* II, 271-289.

where he was or when he would be back. Complaining of lack of funds and shortages of supplies, Emory was uncertain of his authority as Surveyor in the absence of the Commissioner; but, as he informed Stuart, he had decided to organize the survey of the Rio Grande and to push ahead with the work.[23]

His first item of business was signing the controversial Bartlett-Conde agreement, which Gray had never "perfected" with his signature. Once having studied the documents at first hand, Emory concluded that Gray's stand was the correct one. He signed the document, according to his orders from Stuart, but appended a proviso stating that the initial point of the boundary as agreed upon was not the decision of the Joint Commission, but of the commssioners alone. To prevent any possible misunderstanding of his signature on the agreement, Emory obtained a statement from Mexican Surveyor Salazar confirming that the compromise point of 32° 22′ north latitude was "agreed upon by the two commissioners, and nothing else." This, said Emory, allowed him to comply with his orders from the Secretary of the Interior, but left the United States free to repudiate the Bartlett-Conde agreement.[24]

With this task out of the way, Emory began organizing the survey of the Rio Grande. To accomplish this, he set up observatories at Frontera, San Elizario, and Eagle Pass, established a supply depot at Presidio, and sent two surveying parties down the Rio Grande working downriver from Eagle Pass. To these actions he persuaded the Mexican Surveyor to agree.[25] With this work underway he sent a runner westward with the hope of

[23]Emory to Stuart, In Camp near El Paso, December 8, 1851, *SED* 119, 79-81.

[24]Emory, *Report,* I, 6-7.

[25]*Ibid.,* 10-11; Emory to Stuart, Frontera, Texas, January 8, 1852, *SED* 119, 475-477.

locating the absent Bartlett. The employees of the Commission, he wrote Stuart, were becoming mutinous because of the "long absence of the commissioner from the work and his unpardonable neglect to furnish money for their payment." Some of these employees had not been paid for eighteen months, a plight Emory bitterly contrasted with Bartlett's "visiting the States of Chihuahua and Sonora, and the Geysers of California . . . with an equipage and corps of attendants . . . ."[26] By August of 1852 he had pushed the survey downriver from El Paso and was headquartered at Ringgold Barracks, only 241 miles from the mouth of the river, when he heard that the long-absent Bartlett had arrived at El Paso. He immediately wrote the Commissioner of the progress that had been made.

At El Paso Bartlett decided to send Lieutenant Whipple to complete the survey of the southern boundary of New Mexico—the Bartlett-Conde line — while he pushed on to Ringgold Barracks to join Emory. However, he learned that no military escort was available at that place to accompany him and his party southeastward; therefore he decided it would be dangerous to make his journey on the American side of the Rio Grande because of the Comanche Indian menace. He elected to travel through northern Mexico in company with a Mexican escort. Bartlett, Dr. Webb, and twenty-two others left El Paso on October 8, crossing the river and heading almost directly south toward Chihuahua City. Ten days later came the only full-scale Indian attack suffered during the entire survey under Bartlett's direction. That morning of October 18 they broke camp at 7:00 a.m. and had proceeded about a mile when the air was rent by piercing war whoops. From a nearby arroyo poured a band of "savages, who numbered between thirty and forty . . ., their

[26]Emory, *Report,* I, 10-11.

lances poised, screaming and yelling, endeavoring to break the line and stampede the mules." However, the teamsters and five Mexican soldiers did not panic. They carefully held their fire, closing up the wagons and steadying the mules. One Mexican herdsman was wounded in a charge and fell from his horse. A young brave, eager to count coup, rushed up and "pierced him to the heart." As the Indian paused to withdraw his lance, several members of Bartlett's party fired at him with fatal results; thus the score was evened at one and one. Shortly afterward, the savages broke off the engagement and headed for nearby hills, closely pursued by mounted members of the American party. The Indians managed to get away because of "the fleetness of their horses and their knowledge of the ground."[27]

No further such incidents slowed the party, and it arrived in Chihuahua City on October 22 after a 270-mile journey from El Paso. General Angél Trias, a past governor of Chihuahua, gave a formal dinner for Bartlett's group. The Commissioner found Trias a cultivated gentleman but one who "detests the Americans as a people."[28] After repairing the wagons and purchasing

[27] Bartlett, *Personal Narrative,* II, 411-414.

[28] *Ibid.,* 426. Trias was born in Chihuahua City in 1809, the son of a presidial officer of the Spanish army. At the age of twenty he went to Europe to complete his education, studying first in Italy and then in France. Returning to Mexico, he stayed in the capital city as a member of the faction headed by General Anastasio Bustamante. At the end of 1834 Trias once again was in Chihuahua City, where his rise was rapid in local politics and his fame spread because of his campaigns against the Indians. In 1839 he was made a lieutenant colonel of the state militia, and the following year he became a colonel. In 1841 he was elected to the national Congress, and two years later he became a senator. Under the government of President Herrera, Trias became governor of Chihuahua and was received with "manifestations of jubilation" by the population. He left office in January of 1846, following which he became a brigadier general in the army opposing the invasion of the Americans. After the victory of Doniphan's Column at Chihuahua City, Trias retreated southward to Mexico City and participated in the battle of Cerro Gordo. Later in the Mexican War, he once more became governor of his state, but was captured by the Americans and imprisoned. After the war he lived

additional mules, Bartlett left Chihuahua City on November 1, proceeding southeastward into the state of Durango and across to Parras and Saltillo, Coahuila. In the latter city Bartlett received word of the election of Franklin Pierce, a Democrat. He probably knew that this would bring about an end to his duties as Boundary Commissioner, the rules of politics being what they were.

From Saltillo the group pushed on to Monterrey, Nuevo León, and arrived at Ringgold Barracks just before Christmas of 1852. There Bartlett met Emory and received that energetic officer's report of the survey of the Rio Grande. The work had been pushed downriver from El Paso as far as Laredo and could be completed easily. However, at this juncture important dispatches arrived from Washington notifying the Commissioner that additional funds for the work were being withheld because of a proviso attached to the appropriation bill which Congress had passed in August of 1852.[29]

From time to time the American Congress had taken notice of the survey in the Southwest. This notice had been triggered by several of the former members of the Commission. John Weller, after his appointment as Commissioner had been revoked by the Whig administration in 1850, had been elected to the Senate as a Democrat from California, and he had proven a bitter critic of all subsequent work. When Colonel John McClellan had returned to Washington early in 1851, he had filed charges against Bartlett accusing the Commissioner of mismanagement and neg-

in Chihuahua City, serving still a third time as governor between March of 1849 and January of 1852. See Francisco R. Almada, "Gobernadores del Estado: Gral. D. Angel Trias," *Boletín de la Socidad Chihuahuense de Estadios Históricos,* III (July and August 1941), 172-188.

[29]Stuart to Bartlett, October 15, 1852, quoted in Bartlett, *Personal Narrative,* II, 514-516.

Apache Indians Attacking the Train and Party

— From Bartlett, Personal Narrative, *II, 412.*

ligence. On June 28, 1852, Senator Weller requested that McClellan's complaints be referred to a committee for investigation.[30] Even earlier, the Senate had asked the Secretary of the Interior for a full report and copies of all documents on the activities of the Commission. These papers were delivered on July 26,[31] and a full-scale investigation of the proceedings of the Boundary Commission began in the Senate Foreign Relations Committee.

Senator James Murray Mason of Virginia, a leading Democrat and a strong expansionist, headed this committee. After careful study, Mason's committee adopted a resolution which, in effect, repudiated the Bartlett-Conde line and censured the Commissioner's work; the resolution stated:

> That the act of John R. Bartlett, Esq., the commissioner on the part of the United States, in disregarding the boundaries laid down on the map which is made a part of the treaty, and in establishing in lieu of one of the said boundaries a parallel of latitude as determined by astronomical observations, *is a departure from the treaty.*[32]

In the House of Representatives it was Volney E. Howard of Texas who carried the fight against the surrender of the Mesilla Valley to the floor of that body. Howard denounced the Bartlett-Conde line as illegal, censured the American Commissioner for making the agreement, and reproved Secretary of the Interior Stuart for protecting Bartlett and dismissing Gray and Colonel Graham. Bartlett, Howard declared, was guilty of trying to give away the "best route" for a railroad to the Pacific.[33] Another

[30] "Weller Resolution," *Congressional Globe,* XXIV (June 28, 1852), 1628.

[31] "Report of the Secretary of the Interior, in relation to the Mexican boundary commission, July, 1852," which was printed as *SED* 119.

[32] "Report of fixing the initial point," *Senate Report* 345, 32 Cong., 1 Sess., 7.

[33] "Speech of the Hon. V. E. Howard, of Texas, in the House of Representatives, July 6, 1852," *Appendix to the Congressional Globe,* XXV, 776-781.

Texan, Senator Thomas Jefferson Rusk, led the crusade against the Bartlett-Conde compromise. Rusk, who had fought by Sam Houston's side in the famous battle at San Jacinto, cried angrily that he would not vote another dollar for the survey until assurances were forthcoming that "the treaty of Guadalupe Hidalgo, and not the negotiations between the Commissioners, is to settle the initial point of the line upon the Rio Grande."[34]

What these Texans were worried about, of course, was securing a southern route for a transcontinental railroad. Agitation for such a railroad was increasing, and the Texans could readily see the multiplicity of material benefits that would result for their state if the eastern terminus for such a line was at San Antonio, Galveston, or Houston. Other Southern representatives were with the Texans on this account, for such a line eventually would be extended eastward, and the entire South would benefit.

The heated words of the Texans on the House and Senate floors had the desired effect. When the deficiency appropriation bill for the fiscal year 1851-1852 was voted, the Boundary Commission was allocated $80,000 — but with the limiting proviso that "nothing herein contained shall be so construed as to sanction a departure from the point on the Rio Grande north of the town called Paso, designated in the said treaty."[35] A complete triumph for those who desired to retain the Mesilla Valley was obtained when the appropriation bill for the fiscal year 1852-1853 was passed. The opponents of the Bartlett-Conde line were able to attach a proviso to that section of the act giving $125,000

[34]"Remarks by Sen. T. J. Rusk on the Mexican Boundary Commission," *Congressional Globe,* XXIV (July 6, 1852), part 2, p. 1660.

[35]See "An Act to supply Deficiencies in the Appropriations for the fiscal year ending the thirtieth of June, one thousand eight hundred and fifty-two," *ibid.,* XXIV, part 3, p. vi.

to the Boundary Commission making it impossible to spend any of the money "until it shall be made to appear to the President of the United States that the southern boundary is not established . . . further north of the town called Paso than the [line] is laid down in Disturnell's map . . . ."[36]

The Secretary of the Interior had no recourse, after reading the proviso to the appropriations bill, but to inform Bartlett that President Fillmore was forced to conclude that the money could not legally be spent. Since all funds from prior appropriations had been expended, Stuart told Bartlett to make no further drafts on the Treasury. The Commissioner was ordered to hold his men together for six more weeks, if possible, when Congress again would be in session — and perhaps amenable to voting funds sufficient to complete the survey of the Rio Grande. If Bartlett was not able to continue for that long, the Secretary wrote, then he was to make the most favorable disposition possible of the government property in his care and return to Washington.[37] This letter, dated October 15, 1852, reached the Commissioner shortly after his arrival at Ringgold Barracks, and he had no recourse after receiving it but to halt the survey. He did not have enough money on hand even to pay the expenses of his men to their homes. He was forced, therefore, to disband the Boundary Commission and to retire from the field. He disposed of the field equipment and the Commission's animals in San Antonio and made his way to Corpus Christi on the Gulf of Mexico.

[36]See "An Act making appropriations for the civil and diplomatic expenses of the Government for the year ending the thirtieth of June, eighteen hundred and fifty-three, and for other purposes," *ibid.*, XXIV, part 3, p. xviii.

[37]Stuart to Bartlett, October 15, 1851, quoted in Bartlett, *Personal Narrative*, II, 514-516.

On this final leg of the journey, Bartlett was accompanied by Major Emory and most of the discharged members of the Commission. The day before arriving at the Texas port city, that is, on December 31, 1852, came one last adventure. Bartlett suddenly noticed that the entire horizon seemed alive "like the waves of the ocean." A wild mustang herd was thundering across the prairie toward the wagons. Quickly the teamsters moved the wagons together, hitching the mules of each team to the vehicle ahead. One of the teams at the front of the train broke its harness and sped off with the mustangs. Some of the teamsters began firing at the lead wild horses, breaking the line of the charge and turning it in another direction. "Fortunately no one was injured," wrote Bartlett, yet he thought it "altogether the most exciting spectacle we had yet witnessed."[38]

On January 8, 1853, Bartlett and the others took passage on the steamer *Louisiana* bound for New Orleans. The boundary survey had come to a halt. Because of the compromise line he had accepted, Bartlett was discredited as the head of the American Commission, and the impending change in national administrations meant that he was through as Commissioner. The final determination of the southern boundary of New Mexico thus had shifted from the hands of the two Commissioners and Surveyors of the Joint Commission and would be settled by the two governments concerned — but not without difficulties.

[38] *Ibid.*, 522-524.

VII

THE FIGHT FOR THE MESILLA STRIP

On August 16, 1850, Mariano Paredes, a representative from Sonora, arose in the Chamber of Deputies in Mexico City and addressed the national assembly with prophetic words:

> I shall not weary the sovereign body of the nation with descriptions of what Sonora is and what it could be, for those who have written of that land have already done so . . . . The reading of these short notes will be sufficient so that no one will doubt but that this state should claim the attention of the entire nation, and that the nation should use its powers of foresight and read, not far off, the shape of things to come, things which will transpire unless vigorous means are taken to avoid another dismemberment of perhaps the sole remaining jewel that remains to the republic . . . .

The Mexican Cession, forced on his nation only two years before, stood clearly in Paredes' mind as an example of what would happen again if the northern frontier, especially his own state of Sonora, was not populated and developed. The old saying that nature abhors a vacuum held true in the region adjacent to the United States, Paredes knew, and he pointed this out to his fellow deputies:

Sonora is divided from the United States only by the Gila River . . . . The strip on the opposite side will soon be populated. Meanwhile, on our side, years will pass without the same thing happening because of laws enacted but impossible to execute. And it is not the laws impossible of execution that will contain the threat which menaces us . . . . The circumstances are extraordinary, and extraordinary must be the means that you adopt. There are two resolutions, according to my judgment, that will not require money . . . . First, a good colonization law; and second, mercantile arrangements . . . .

Paredes went on to spell out exactly what he had in mind, and to present these proposals in the form of recommended legislation. A colonization law written especially to suit conditions in Sonora was the first necessity he dwelt upon. He pointed out that already aggressive Americans were casting covetous eyes on his state and on Baja California.[1] These Americans, Paredes contended, knew that Sonora contained "equal or more precious metals than those that today are mined in Upper California." He drew the deputies a picture of the potential of his state: "Sonora, since the last century, has produced and is producing both gold and silver. The fertility of its lands near the boundary is beyond doubt." What was needed to develop both the mineral and agricultural potential was people — people who would come to the state and "make it great, and . . . put up a barrier to [American] ambition." Paredes thereupon introduced a proposed law which

[1]Robles, *Memoria del Secretario de Estado,* 16-22, carries additional details of this filibustering activity, and shows the Mexican government's point of view. Interestingly, Paredes himself was partly responsible for some of it. In 1850 this Sonoran deputy had suggested that Sonorans might appeal to the United States for assistance in dealing with the Apaches if Mexico City did not offer help; although this movement was abortive, it did have contacts in California which gave impetus to the first filibustering expedition from California to Mexico. See Rufus K. Wyllys, *The French in Sonora, 1850-1854* (Berkeley: University of California Press, 1932), 52.

spelled out in great detail how the colonization should be stimulated.

Article one of the law declared, "The frontiers of Sonora are suitable for colonization, especially that land adjacent to the Gila." The next article drew a line north of which he wished to see populated. Paredes would have the Chamber declare open to colonization all land north of a line drawn two leagues (approximately 5.2 miles) beyond the Spanish presidial cordon as established by the Royal Regulations of 1772. The land north of this line would be offered to colonists, either Mexican or European, to whom would be guaranteed "their properties and dearest liberties," and to whom would be offered the following inducements:

1. To each colonist, either European or Mexican, and a farmer by trade, will be given at no charge, cost, or obligation irrigable land a *labor* (approximately 177 acres) . . . or double that amount in temporarily usable or dry land.

2. To those who are devoted exclusively to raising cattle [will be given] a *sitio* (approximately 4,428 acres) in level land . . . or double this amount in mountainous or broken land.

3. In the towns that are formed, they will be given a town lot on which to build their homes . . . .

4. Each colonist who plans to settle may introduce at the port of Guaymas and duty free all the necessities of agriculture, transport, trade, and arts, and they may also bring in duty free, one time only, merchandise to the value of two hundred pesos . . . . This tax remission may only be received at the Guaymas customs house . . . .

5. If there are empresarios for the transport of European colonists, the nation will grant them for each one hundred male colonists over twenty years of age that settle in such colonies two town lots . . ., two *labors* of irrigable land, two non-irrigable fields, and ten *sitios* for stock raising; moreover, for each one hundred male colonists settled, upon certification from the leader of the colony, the Guaymas customs house will remit 250 pesos . . . .

Amiel W. Whipple

— *From Miller (ed.),* Photographic History of the Civil War, *X, 131.*

In return for these privileges and grants, each colonist had to become a Mexican citizen, swear to defend his adopted country from "barbarians of all types," enlist in the militia, and hold the land for eight years before selling. Any colonist that failed to comply with these obligations would be "declared unworthy of social confidence, and his properties shall revert to the nation."

Paredes proposed in his law that a commission be created to map northern Sonora and divide it into townships. This commission would be composed of two civil engineers, two brigadier generals with topographical experience, the commanding general of Sonora, and one or two commissioners named by the governor of that state. This commission, after surveying the land, would reside either in Tucson or Fronteras until the first new town was formed; then the commission would move there and exercise jurisdiction over the colonization. As a town was formed, it would be under a "special leader, named as a military governor." When a town reached one thousand inhabitants, it had the privilege of naming its "authorities for the administration of justice, the leader of the colony exercising the functions of political prefect." When the town reached a population of five thousand inhabitants, it would be "incorporated into the state of Sonora" and have the same status as all other towns designated as municipalities.

To avoid the neglect that accompanied state supervision, Paredes concluded part one of his proposed law by stating: "The government of the nation shall remain in charge [of the colonization], exercising the strictest responsibility in seeing that the monthly necessities of the committee in charge of the colonies are satisfied punctually so that the interested parties may not suffer miseries in such remote places."

Section two of Paredes' recommended legislation was designed to encourage mercantile development. The Sonoran deputy urged that Guaymas be declared a duty-free port for twenty-five years. The removal of all export and import duties would attract men with capital to Sonora, he declared; there they would develop business and industry. Businessmen were removed from politics, he said, and thus would serve as a counter-balance to politically ambitious creators of chaos. The new businesses and industries would aid in increasing the population, thus serving still further to counter the threat of the United States coming back for another slice of the *patria.* Paredes concluded by begging the chamber's forgiveness for the length of his talk and of his two projected laws. "I am certain it contains many errors," he said, "but I am confident of the rectitude and purity of my intentions."[2]

Despite the sincerity of Paredes' speech — and the good sense it showed — nothing was done by the Chamber of Deputies, just as likewise nothing had been done two years earlier when the idea of frontier colonization had first been suggested. On July 20, 1848, Mariano Arista, then Secretary of War and Marine (and president of Mexico from 1850 to 1853), had promulgated a decree entitled "Military Colonies. Project for their Establishment on the Eastern and Western Frontiers of the Republic." This decree projected a series of military colonies from Baja California to Tamaulipas along the new boundary between the United States and Mexico "in order to preserve the integrity of our territory, as well as to defend the frontier states from the frequent and cruel incursions of the barbarians." This

[2]M. Paredes, *Proyectos de leyes sobre Colonización y Comercio en el Estado de Sonora* (Mexico City: I. Cumplido, 1850), 1-24.

plan carried the sanction of José Joaquin de Herrera, the president of Mexico in 1848.

To accomplish the goal of a series of military colonies, the decree provided that such settlements would be under the direct supervision of the general government, not the individual states. The frontier would be divided into three districts: Frontera de Oriente, consisting of those colonies in Tamaulipas and Coahuila; Chihuahua; and Frontera de Occidente, consisting of those colonies in Baja California and Sonora. In command of each district would be a colonel, who would function with all the powers of a commandant-general — *i.e.,* he would have civil, judicial, and military powers. Most of these colonies would have 150 soldiers, although some would have less; a normal complement would consist of 40 infantrymen and 110 cavalry troops, along with three pieces of artillery. Whenever a colony grew to sufficient size to qualify for status as a pueblo (a town with self-governing rights), it would then be placed under the jurisdiction of the state wherein it was built, and would cease to be a military colony.[3] This decree, in essence was a corollary to the Spanish Royal Regulations of Presidios which had been promulgated in 1772 and which the Mexican government had continued to use as a guideline for the frontier between 1821 and 1848.[4]

Although Paredes' speech resulted in no new laws to encourage immigration, and Guaymas was not made a free port, it did cause a few intelligent men to give serious thought to the aggres-

[3]Mariano Arista, *Colonias Militares. Proyecto para su Establecimiento en las Fronteras de Oriente y Occidente de la Republica* (Mexico City: I. Cumplido, 1848).

[4]For a study of the Spanish military system in the Southwest, as well as a copy of the Royal Regulations, see Sidney B. Brinckerhoff and Odie B. Faulk, *Lancers for the King* (Phoenix: Arizona Historical Foundation, 1965).

Valley and Town of Mesilla, New Mexico

— *By Charles Shuchard, from* The A. B. Gray Report.

siveness of the American frontiersmen and the attractiveness of the Mexican frontier because of its natural resources and small population. On January 7, 1851, a junta created by the Minister of Relations,[5] José María Lecunza, presented a report wherein it recommended not only the colonization of Sonora but also of the entire northern tier of states and the Territory of Baja California, as suggested by Arista's decree. "The time has arrived," stated the junta, "when inactivity in regularizing and facilitating foreign immigration and colonization is going to be very deplorable for the republic." Agriculture should be encouraged, for the export of farm products would be a source of wealth, it continued. The miners of Upper California were paying extremely high prices for anything edible; why should Mexico not cash in on this potential bonanza? And in the cities, manufacturing should develop. Action was needed, the junta declared.[6]

Still nothing was done, even though the boundary survey was not proceeding satisfactorily. Finally on January 26, 1852, the venerable Senator Juan Nepomuceno Almonte, a diplomat whose service to his country was above reproach, spoke to the national senate on the subject of colonization: "The situation of the states of Chihuahua, Durango, Nuevo Leon, Tamaulipas, Zacatecas, Sonora and even Sinaloa could not be more deplorable, for daily its inhabitants are assassinated, its haciendas plundered, and its fields burned by the various tribes of barbarians who ceaselessly invade that area." The answer to all the problems of the area was getting additional people to move there, he said. The United States had attracted immigrants to its frontier from Europe by pointing out the advantages of moving there; why

[5]A cabinet post corresponding to the American Secretary of State.

[6]See *Memoria que la dirreccion de Colonizacion é Industria* (Mexico City: G. Torkes, 1851).

should Mexico not do the same? Both Mexican and European settlers should be urged to move to the north, he argued, for thereby the barbarians would be halted at no cost to the central government — and at the same time forming a barrier to further American aggression. Almonte went on to spell out the method of financing this venture and he indicated the need for advertising in the various European periodicals. Mexico, he thought, should not rest until it had a population of 25,000,000.[7]

Time ran out for Mexico before anything was done, however. The Bartlett-Conde line was rejected by the American Congress in the summer of 1852. The disbandment of the American Commission in December of that year left the southern boundary of New Mexico as yet undefined and still to be definitively set. Unsettled, also, was the ownership of the so-called Mesilla Strip — the disputed six thousand square miles of territory between 31° 52′ north latitude and 32° 22′ north latitude and extending westward for some 175 miles. One factor complicating any settlement of this problem was the attitude of the inhabitants of the little town of Mesilla in the disputed area. According to John Russell Bartlett, the discredited American Commissioner, the settlers at Mesilla had moved there from Santa Fe and other New Mexican towns after the Treaty of Guadalupe Hidalgo was concluded in order to escape American jurisdiction.

William Carr Lane, governor of New Mexico, insisted that the people of the Mesilla area wished to be American citizens and that they had sent him a petition asking to be retained in the United States.[8] Lane was a native of Pennsylvania, born near

[7] Juan Nepomuceno Almonte, *Proyectos de Leyes sobre Colonizacion* (Mexico City: Ignacio Cumplido, 1852).

[8] Rippy, *The United States and Mexico,* 111-116.

Brownsville in 1789. He had studied at Jefferson and Dickinson colleges, and had received his M.D. from the University of Pennsylvania. Afterward, he moved to Missouri where he practiced medicine and served in the state legislature. In 1832 he was elected mayor of St. Louis, a position to which he was reelected eight times. According to one historian, he was offered Thomas Hart Benton's seat in the U.S. Senate, but refused. He accepted the post of governor of New Mexico probably because he wanted to leave St. Louis following the death of his son. Sworn in as governor on September 13, 1852, he almost immediately had difficulty with the military commander of the Department of New Mexico, Colonel Edwin V. Sumner. Quarrels with military officials and Indian depredations caused the new governor no end of trouble, but he still had time to take note of what he considered an incursion on American territory.[9]

Governor Lane became incensed over the Mesilla question when he learned that Governor Angél Trias of Chihuahua had sent five hundred men and six to eight pieces of artillery to Mesilla. Trias had to withdraw this force within a short time because he lacked the funds to maintain them.[10] When Lane learned that Congress seemingly had repudiated the Bartlett-Conde compromise line by attaching a proviso to the appropriated funds of the Boundary Commission, he called on Colonel Sumner for aid in asserting the jurisdiction of the United States over the Mesilla Valley. Sumner refused to help, however, since he had no orders from his military superiors to do so; besides,

[9]For a biographical sketch of Governor Lane, see Horn, *New Mexico's Troubled Years*, 36-49.

[10]Gray, *Report*, 25. The Surveyor stated that the Mexican commissioner for the state of Chihuahua, Jacques y Zuloazue, had admitted in correspondence to Governor Lane of New Mexico that Chihuahua had not extended its jurisdiction to the Mesilla Valley "until Messrs. Bartlett and Conde had agreed to establish the boundary on the parallel of 32 degrees 22 minutes latitude."

he did not like Lane. The governor thereupon began gathering a group of New Mexican civilians, augmented by volunteers from Texas, to take control of the area by force. On February 15, 1853, Lane wrote his wife:

> Be not surprised if I should take possession of the disputed territory, which I dare say I will find to be without adequate protection, against internal and external violence . . . . If duty calls upon me to occupy and protect this country, provisionally, until the line shall be definitely established, I will do it . . . .[11]

Lane led his volunteers to the village of Doña Ana. There on March 13 he issued a proclamation:

> I, William Carr Lane, Governor of the Territory of New Mexico (upon my official responsibility and without orders from the cabinet at Washington) do hereby, in behalf of the United States, retake possession of the said disputed territory to be held provisionally by the United States until the question of boundary shall be determined by the United States and the Mexican Republic . . . .[12]

He stated that the disputed area had been a part of New Mexico from 1825 to 1851; that it had been seized illegally by the governor of Chihuahua in 1851;[13] that Chihuahua had failed to bring good government or to secure the rights of person, property, or conscience, or to protect the citizens of the Mesilla Valley from the Indians; that revolutionary conditions in Mexico caused the state of Chihuahua to be unable to guarantee these rights or protection in the future; that most of the people of the

[11]Quoted in Horn, *New Mexico's Troubled Years,* 47.

[12]Governor William Carr Lane to J. L. Taylor, Santa Fe, January 23, 1854, *House Report* 81, 33 Cong., 1 Sess., 1-2.

[13]In his diary, under the date September 2, 1853, Governor Lane wrote his personal opinion of John Russell Bartlett: "No doubt now remains, on my mind, that this quondam Boundary Commissioner, is both Fool & Knave . . . ." See William G. B. Carson (ed.), "William Carr Lane, Diary," *New Mexico Historical Review,* XXXIX (October 1964), 300.

valley wanted the protection and jurisdiction of the United States; and that the United States was governing the area and would continue to do so.[14]

In Chihuahua City certain state officials also had been keeping a close watch on events to the north, especially the gathering of a volunteer force by Lane to march to Mesilla. In February of 1853 this concern reached such a high pitch that the state legislature declared a state of emergency and recalled General Angél Trias to the governorship. Trias responded to the Lane proclamation by issuing his own manifesto. He asserted that Chihuahua had owned that region since time immemorial; that the boundary had legally been set at 32° 22′; that Chihuahua had occupied the area without opposition in 1851 "under the watch of officials of the United States who were not accustomed to remaining silent in cases in which [American] rights were in doubt;" and that it was the desire of the people of the area to belong to Mexico. Finally he said directly to Lane, "I will make use of all necessary means for the defense and preservation of the territory of La Mesilla in case of an attack and the responsibility will rest exclusively on Your Excellency for the consequences . . . ."[15] Francisco R. Almada, a prominent twentieth-century historian of northern Mexico declared of this action by Trias: "In the answer of Governor Trias to the proclamation of the intruders can be seen concepts surrounded by patriotism and of dignity, defending the rights of Mexico and of the state of Chihuahua . . . ."[16]

Actions followed words on both sides. Trias, having expressed his claim to the area, next strengthened his garrison at El Paso,

[14]Lane to Taylor, Santa Fe, January 23, 1854, *House Report* 81, 33 Cong., 1 Sess., 1-2.

[15]Ochoa, *Integración y Desintegración,* 130-131.

[16]Almada, "Gral. D. Angel Trias," *Boletín,* 179.

and he notified the Secretary of Relations of the incidents. The Mexican government approved Trias' actions; it sent two emissaries to the area, and it ordered the militia put under arms to aid the regulars. Thus Trias had at his disposal a brigade, labelled the Trias Brigade, with which he marched toward El Paso during the first week in April. Lane again called on Sumner for aid, but again was rebuffed. Therefore he appealed directly to the White House for help. When Alfred Conkling, American ambassador to Mexico, protested the New Mexican governor's actions, Lane replied indignantly that he had been "appointed Governor of all New Mexico, and not a part."[17]

With the governors of New Mexico and Chihuahua organizing militias and issuing bellicose proclamations, a second war appeared imminent between the United States and its southern neighbor. Peace between the two nations had been declared four years previously, but the disputed boundary seemed destined to shatter the tenuous good relations that had been established and to plunge the two into battle once again. Mexico's foreign minister began sending directives to that nation's diplomatic agents abroad instructing them to seek aid from European nations in case of war with the United States.[18] Just at that critical juncture, however, both nations took a second and hard look at the situation.

[17]Quoted in Paul Neff Garber, *The Gadsden Treaty* (Gloucester, Massachusetts: Peter Smith, 1959), 71.

[18]See "Circular to the Mexican diplomatic agents abroad with respect to securing aid of England, France, and Spain to 'restrain the ambitious designs' of the United," and "Circular to the diplomatic agents abroad instructing them to secure aid, direct or indirect, for Mexico in case of hostilities with the United States, January 20, 1854," in boxes labeled 1853 and 1854-55, First Series, International Affairs, as cited in Herbert E. Bolton, *Guide to the Materials for the History of the United States in the Principal Archives of Mexico* (Washington, 1913), 229-230.

The Treaty of Guadalupe Hidalgo, especially the cession of land to the United States, had been a bitter and galling humiliation to Mexican pride. But the war had left the nation no recourse but acceptance. For the five years following the end of this conflict, there had been a singular absence of *pronuncimientos* against the government, and the democratic process was allowed to function. José Joaquin Herrera had been restored to the office of president in June of 1848, and two years later came the first peaceful transfer of authority since the winning of independence. Mariano Arista, an honest and capable administrator who had been serving as Secretary of War and Marine, came into office in 1850 and worked to reduce army expenditures, to consolidate the foreign debt, and to stabilize the economy. The conservative party, which had strong monarchial tendencies, still was a potent force, however, and in January of 1853 it managed to overthrow Arista. The leaders of this party thereupon elected Antonio López de Santa Anna, the hero — or villain — of so many episodes of Mexican history, to be dictator for one year. Santa Anna returned from his exile in Venezuela on April 1, 1853, and was installed in office on the twentieth of that month. A close appraisal of the Mesilla dispute convinced the wily dictator that his most pressing need was money, not a war in which victory was unlikely. To stay in power he had to have "silver cannonballs" — *i.e.*, money to shoot to this and to that general to keep the soldiers loyal to his regime. Diplomacy seemed much more likely to produce these funds than battle.[19]

In Washington, D.C., the appraisal likewise was closely connected with the realities of practical politics. The newly elected

[19]Wilfrid Hardy Callcott, *Santa Anna: The Story of an Enigma Who Once Was Mexico* (Norman: University of Oklahoma Press, 1936), 278-285; Clarence R. Wharton, *El Presidente: A Sketch of the Life of General Santa Anna* (Austin, Texas: Gammel's Book Store, 1926), 182-184.

administration of Franklin Pierce took office in March of 1853, and immediately it was faced with the problem of the disputed boundary. President Pierce flatly denounced the Mexican claim to the Mesilla Valley. Fortunately for the president, however, the question of Governor Lane's impetuousness solved itself; in the summer of 1853 Lane resigned to make what would prove to be an unsuccessful bid to be elected Congressional delegate from New Mexico. The new appointee to that office was David Meriwether,[20] who went to his post with orders to improve relations with Mexico. Pierce and his close advisors did not want a war, for they knew that another conflict with Mexico would probably result in the ruin of the Democratic party, and it would even imperil the Union itself. New Englanders had protested violently against the war of 1846-1848, and there was every reason to believe they would prove even more hostile to another such conflict in 1853.[21]

As a result of these considerations, both the United States and Mexico were in a mood suddenly to remember and accede to the provisions of Article XXI of the Treaty of Guadalupe Hidalgo, which stated:

> If unhappily any disagreement should hereafter arise between the Governments of the two Republics, whether with respect to the interpretation of any stipulation in this treaty, or with respect to any other particular concerning the political or commercial relations of the two Nations, the said Governments, in the name of those Nations, do promise to each other, that they will endeavour in the most sincere and earnest manner, to settle the differences so arising, and to preserve the state of peace and friendship, in which the two countries are now placing themselves; using, for this end, mutual representations and pacific negotiations.[22]

[20]For a biographical sketch of David Meriwether, see Horn, *New Mexico's Troubled Years,* 52-71.

[21]Rippy, *The United States and Mexico,* 127.

[22]Malloy, *Treaties,* 1113.

Ringgold Barracks and Rio Grande City

— *From Emory,* Report, *Part I, page 63.*

William H. Emory

—*From Francis T. Miller (ed.),*
The Photographic History of the Civil War,
(New York, 1911-1912), X, 191.

VIII

THE GADSDEN PURCHASE

JAMES GADSDEN'S name has been inseparably linked with the Southwest because of the treaty which he negotiated and which he signed in Mexico City in December of 1853. His background was such, however, that his personal knowledge of the area was about as limited as that of John Russell Bartlett. Born in Charleston, South Carolina, in 1788, he graduated from Yale University in 1806, then returned to his native city to go into business. Commercial activity apparently did not appeal to him, for soon thereafter he entered the Army, where he stayed for more than a decade, fighting in the War of 1812 and the Seminole War. Despite the fact that he rose to the rank of colonel, he resigned his commission in 1821 and went to Florida. There he served in the territorial legislature and as federal commissioner for the removal of the Seminole Indians. In 1839 he returned to Charleston where a year later he became president of the Louisville, Cincinnati and Charleston Railroad, a position he held for ten years. The road had only a few miles of track and a three-million-dollar debt, but Gadsden dreamed of consolidating the many short lines in the South into a regional system that would show a profit. This he would use as a base for building a transcontinental line to the Pacific Coast. By the early 1850's he had decided that the Gila River route was the most promising way to realize his dream, and was actively promoting it. But the disputed boundary of southern New Mexico made such a dream remote of realization, and an additional acquisition of land from Mexico would be a necessity, he felt.

When the Franklin Pierce administration took office in March of 1853, the new Secretary of War was the former Senator from Mississippi, Jefferson Davis. Through the influence of Davis, who was dissatisfied with the territorial acquisitions at the end of the Mexican War and wanted still more land to the south, Gadsden in May of 1853 was named minister to Mexico.[1] Davis' use of influence is somewhat surprising in view of the fact that Gadsden was not an ardent expansionist; during the Mexican War Gadsden had spoken out against annexing a large slice of Mexico, and by 1853 his viewpoint had changed but little. He did believe that the line as drawn in the Treaty of Guadalupe Hidalgo was not based sufficiently on geography, that both nations should work to draw a natural boundary. However, such a new boundary, he felt, would have to be at Mexico's expense.[2]

Immediately after his appointment Gadsden began to gather information about Mexico. A free trader, he felt that the United States should promote closer commercial ties with the republic to the south. Knowing that he would be required to negotiate a new boundary, Gadsden also sought information about the

[1]Davis wrote Gadsden of the appointment even before Secretary of State William L. Marcy officially communicated the news, and Gadsden corresponded with Davis during the time he was in Mexico City negotiating. See Garber, *The Gadsden Treaty,* 81.

[2]*Ibid.*

border country. He wanted no future revision to be necessary once a new settlement was made. For information he turned to former Surveyor Andrew B. Gray. The two held lengthy discussions, especially concerning what land would be necessary for a southern transcontinental railroad.[3]

On July 15 Secretary of State William L. Marcy delivered to Gadsden a set of official instructions for negotiating a settlement of the boundary dispute with Mexico. In addition, however, Gadsden was to settle all outstanding difficulties between the two nations. Marcy admitted that Mexicans were embittered against the United States by the recent war, but that the new minister should emphasize the friendship of Americans for the people of Mexico. Gadsden was to secure a release from Article XI of the Treaty of Guadalupe Hidalgo — *i.e.,* a release from financial liability for the raids of Indians living in the United States and plundering in Mexico; he was to establish the rights of American citizens crossing the Isthmus of Tehuantepec, and he was to achieve a resumption of commerce between the two republics. But his primary goal was to secure sufficient land for the buliding of a transcontinental railroad. For such an accomodation, the United States "would be willing to pay liberally." About the disputed Mesilla Strip, Gadsden was told not to press the American right to this area if Mexico proved willing to negotiate a new boundary.[4] Should the matter become of importance, however, he was to state that the Bartlett-Conde compromise line was an illegal settlement since Lieutenant A. W.

[3]*Ibid.,* 83.

[4]These instructions are contained in David Hunter Miller (ed.), *Treaties and Other International Acts of the United States of America* (8 vols., Washington, 1942-1948), VI, 342-347. Portions of the instructions are in William R. Manning, *Diplomatic Correspondence of the United States: Inter-American Affairs, 1831-1860* (12 vols., Washington, 1932-1937), IX, 607-609, 616-621.

Whipple's signature as Surveyor *ad interim* on the document was meaningless.[5]

Gadsden arrived in Mexico City on August 4, and held his first conference with President Santa Anna thirteen days later. Then on August 20 the serious business of negotiating began between Gadsden and Manuel Diaz de Bonilla, the Mexican Minister of Foreign Relations. The result of their meetings of the following three weeks, which were concerned primarily with Indian depredations and the American liability under Article XI, was a stalemate; Gadsden contended that since the United States did not pay its own citizens for such damages, it certainly did not owe Mexico anything for them. On September 25 the American minister met with Santa Anna, at which time the question of the boundary was discussed. Santa Anna agreed at that meeting to the negotiations of a new boundary between the two countries; as for the disputed Mesilla area, they agreed that it would remain as it was until a new boundary was set. This agreement stopped all threat of war between Mexico and the United States.[6] On October 3 Gadsden wrote Marcy that he felt a treaty could be concluded reconciling all areas of dispute between the United States and Mexico, but such a settlement "must be paid for."[7]

Gadsden's reports to Marcy stressed the political instability in Mexico and the constant threat of a new revolution. Marcy decided that the United States had best act with dispatch, for a golden opportunity to negotiate might be lost if Santa Anna were overthrown. Therefore on October 22 the Secretary of State sent a special messenger, Christopher L. Ward, with memorized

[5]Garber, *The Gadsden Treaty,* 83-85; Rippy, *The United States and Mexico,* 128.

[6]Garber, *The Gadsden Treaty,* 86-87.

[7]*Ibid.,* 89.

instructions to Mexico. These instructions revolved around the possible boundary between the United States and Mexico. Preferred by President Pierce was offer number one: $50,000,000 would be paid for a boundary that would give the United States the northern part of Coahuilla, Chihuahua, Sonora, and all of Baja California. Offer number two was $35,000,000 with a boundary farther north that did not include Baja California; offer number three was $30,000,000 with the line still farther north but included Baja; the fourth offer was the same line as number three but excluding Baja, for which $20,000,000 would be paid. If none of these offers was acceptable to Mexico, then Gadsden was to get sufficient territory for a transcontinental railroad; the suggestion was that such a boundary should be 31° 48′ from the Rio Grande to the Gulf of California. For this and a release from Article XI, Gadsden was authorized to offer up to $15,000,000.[8]

Ward delivered these instructions to Gadsden on November 14, and Gadsden proceeded to negotiate with authority. However, the Mexican government seemed reluctant to discuss the sale of a large amount of land, and gradually Gadsden was driven to accept the least desirable of his offers — sufficient only for a transcontinental railroad. Santa Anna later said that the American minister told him that the disputed land was necessary for a railroad to facilitate communication with California. According to the wily dictator's later account, Gadsden told him that if Mexico negotiated it would receive a "good indemnity;" if Mexico would not negotiate then "imperious necessity would compel [the United States] to occupy it one way or another."[9]

[8] *Ibid.*, 91-93. See also Miller, *Treaties*, VI, 361-362.

[9] J. Fred Rippy, "A Ray of Light on the Gadsden Purchase," *Southwestern Historical Quarterly*, XXIV (January 1921), 238.

According to Santa Anna's memoirs, the conversation was not cordial: Gadsden said, "The projected railroad from New York to California must be built by way of the Mesilla Valley, because there is no other feasible route. The Mexican government will be splendidly indemnified. The valley must belong to the United States by an indemnity, or we will take it."

"Naturally," wrote Santa Anna, "such talk aroused my wrath, and I said, 'Mr. Gadsden, I heard you say Splendid Indemnity, and am anxious to know how much it will amount to."[10] The answer of $15,000,000 apparently cooled Santa Anna's wrath, and on December 30 a "Treaty of Boundary and Cession of Territory" was signed by the American minister and Mexican plenipotentiaries. Article I of the agreement set the new boundary: from the juncture of the Gila and Colorado rivers, the boundary would run down the middle of the Colorado to a point six miles above the head of the Gulf of California, then in a direct line to the intersection of the 31st parallel with the 111th degree of longitude, and thence in a straight line to the middle of the Rio Grande at 31° 47′ 30″ some eight miles north of El Paso del Norte. Article II of the treaty absolved the United States of all responsibility under Article XI of the Treaty of Guadalupe Hidalgo. Other articles provided for American navigation of the Gulf of California and the Colorado River, the organization of a claims commission, and the promise of mutual cooperation in suppressing filibustering expeditions. For this cession of land the United States agreed to pay Mexico $15,000,000. Ratifications of the treaty were to be exchanged within six months,[11] a very short period of time but Santa Anna desperately needed the money.

[10]Quoted in Wharton, *El Presidente,* 189.

[11]This treaty is in Miller, *Treaties,* VI, 318-322.

When the news of this treaty spread in the United States, comment split according to sectional interests. The North denounced it, while the South spoke in favor of it. President Pierce was unhappy with the agreement because it did not get as much of Mexico as he wanted, but at the urging of Davis and Marcy he consented to send it to the Senate for ratification or rejection. On February 10, 1854, the Senate began considering the treaty — a most unfortunate time in view of the fact that the Kansas-Nebraska Bill was then before the body and was causing the pro- and anti-slavery factions to gird themselves for mortal combat. The greatest amount of debate, of course, came over the first article wherein the new boundary was spelled out. One by one the amendments offered by expansionists were defeated. Then Senator James Murray Mason of Virginia, who favored the treaty, offered a new boundary line. He proposed that the boundary begin in the middle of the Rio Grande at 31° 47′ north latitude, run due west for one hundred miles, turn due south to 31° 20′, proceeded due west to the point where it intersected the 111th meidian, then went in a straight line to a point in the middle of the Colorado River twenty English miles (approximately twenty-eight miles) below its junction with the Gila. It then proceeded up the middle of the Colorado until it met the line dividing Upper and Lower California.

The original Gadsden Treaty had called for the payment of $15,000,000 for the ceded land, and the United States agreed to assume up to $5,000,000 of the claims of Americans against Mexico. Amendments were offered — and accepted — which changed both these particulars. The total amount to be paid for the ceded land was scaled down to $10,000,000, which would be paid in two installments. The first payment of $7,000,000 would be given Mexico upon its ratification of the amended treaty; the final installment of $3,000,000 would be paid when the boundary survey was completed. On the question of the United States assuming a liability for $5,000,000 in claims,[12] this entire provision was stricken; instead the Senate included the clause abrogating Article XI of the Treaty of Guadalupe Hidalgo, thus extinguishing Mexican claims against the United States but leaving intact American claims against Mexico.

On April 17 a vote was taken on the amended Gadsden Treaty. It failed to receive the necessary two-thirds vote, for only twenty-seven were in favor to eighteen against. To secure additional support, proponents of the treaty thereupon added a new amendment relating to the right of transit on the Isthmus of Tehuantepec:

> The Mexican government having on the 5th of February, 1853, authorized the construction of a plank and rail road across the Isthmus of Tehuantepec, and to secure stable benefits of said transit way to the persons and merchandise of the citizens of Mexico and the United States it is stipulated that neither government will interpose any obstacle to the transit of persons and merchandise of both nations; and at no time shall higher charges be made on the persons and property of foreign nations, nor shall any interest in said transit way, nor in the proceeds thereof, be transferred to any foreign government.[13]

This clause greatly pleased many Senators because it guaranteed a vital route to California; until a transcontinental railroad was completed in the United States, much of the traffic to the Pacific Coastal area would be overland. When the amended treaty came

[12]For the Mexican side of this dispute over Indian raids, see Luis G. Zorrilla, *Historia de las Relaciones entre Mexico y Los Estados Unidos de America, 1800-1958* (2 vols., Mexico City: Editorial Porrua, 1965-1966), I, 275-292.

[13]For this Article, as well as all other parts of the completed treaty, see *ibid.*, 293-302.

to a vote on April 25, it passed by a comfortable margin—thirty-three to twelve.[14]

The lasting mystery of the Gadsden Treaty is why Senator Mason drew just the boundary he did to divide the United States and Mexico. The first portion of the boundary—*i.e.,* beginning at 31° 47′ north latitude and proceeding west for one hundred miles, then running due south to 31° 20′ north latitude, and then going west was deliberately drawn in the hope of securing the entirety of Cooke's Wagon Road for the United States. This road, laid out by Philip St. George Cooke during the Mexican War, had subsequently become a major route to California and was known as the Gila Trail. The remaining portion of the boundary was actually drawn by Mexican diplomats. Pierce's instructions to Gadsden had been to secure a line that would insure the United States a port on the Gulf of California. The least desirable of the five proposals Gadsden was empowered to make was a boundary commencing on the Rio Grande at 31° 48′ and running west to the Gulf of California. Baja California would not have been included in the new American territory. Even the most inexperienced diplomat could readily see that what would result for Mexico eventually would be the loss of Baja California under such an arrangement. Filibustering activity was already underway in that area, and non-contiguous territory would be lost very shortly unless changes were made. The Mexican Foreign Minister, Manuel Diaz de Bonilla, convinced Gadsden that Mexico would never agree to a sale that did not include a land access route to Baja. The original Gadsden Treaty had provided for a boundary six miles above the mouth of the Colorado; during the months when the treaty was under consideration in the United States Senate, the Mexican

[14]Garber, *The Gadsden Treaty,* 131.

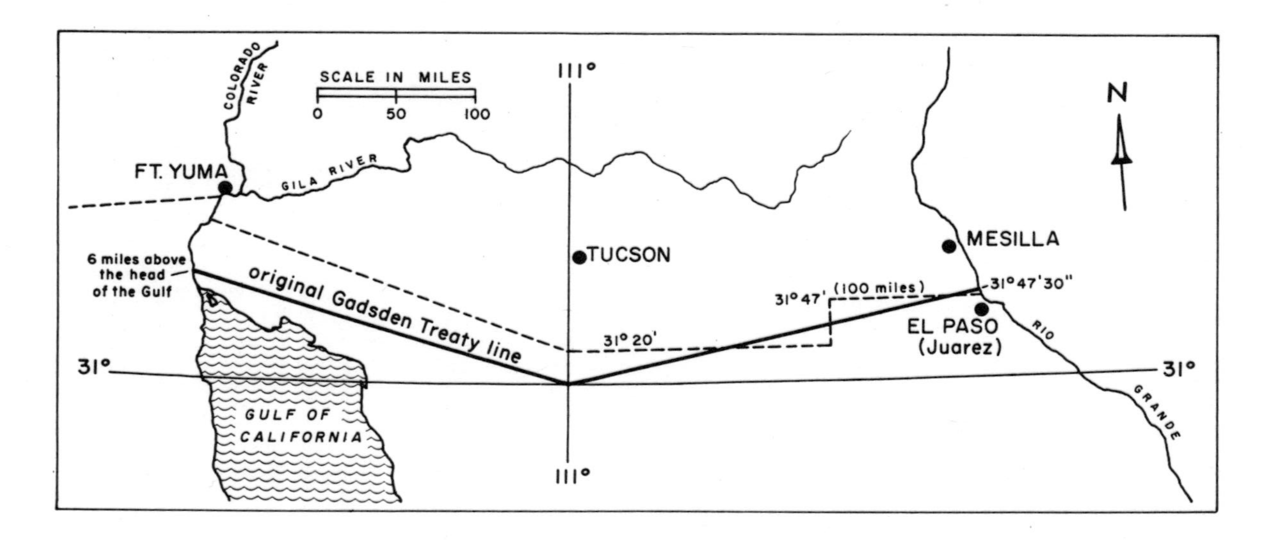

—*Drawn by Don Bufkin.*

minister in Washington, Juan Nepomuceno Almonte, who had strongly urged his nation to colonize the northern frontier, was actively working to convince influential Senators that Mexico should have a land-bridge to Baja. What he sold these influential Senators was the boundary he had drawn in 1852 to accompany his pamphlet on colonization, *Proyectos de Leyes Sobre Colonizacion,* which gave Mexico far more than the six miles allowed by the original Gadsden Treaty.[15] Almonte's wishes became law in the final version of the treaty as passed by the Senate.

James Gadsden was so dissatisfied with the amended version of his treaty which passed the Senate that he went to Mexico in the hope of seeing it defeated there. However, he soon relented for he realized that any new treaty which might be negotiated would probably never be ratified by the American Senate, which was so divided by the slavery question. President Santa Anna, however, had no doubts whatsoever about the amended treaty; he had to accept it in order to get the first payment of seven million dollars, money which was desperately needed by his regime if it was to sustain itself in power. Besides, Ambassador Almonte wrote from Washington that a Mexican rejection of the treaty doubtless would mean a war with the United States. Santa Anna therefore signed the amended treaty of May 31.[16] Late in life the Mexican president wrote that he had accepted the agreement because he "recognized that it was impolitic to refuse their [the United States'] consent, there remaining the satisfaction of

[15]See Ochoa, *Integración y Desintegración,* 135; Rippy, *The United States and Mexico* 151-152; Garber, *The Gadsden Treaty,* 123-125; William R. Matthews, "An Answer to a Century-Old Question," Tucson *Arizona Daily Star,* September 15, 1965, Section F, page 10; and Zorrilla, *Historia de las Relaciones,* I, 351-354.

[16]Garber, *The Gadsden Treaty,* 139.

having obtained for a piece of wild country relatively what they gave for half of the national property."[17]

In June the Gadsden Treaty was sent to the House of Representatives in Washington. There it was referred to the Ways and Means Committee for the drafting of a bill to appropriate the funds necessary for paying Mexico the first installment of the $10,000,000. In the House the bill was subjected to the same debate by members of both the pro- and anti-slavery factions. In addition, it became embroiled in still another variation of the sectional feuding — Thomas Hart Benton, formerly a Senator and now a revered and respected member of the Lower House, spoke heatedly against the measure because he feared the transcontinental railroad would indeed take a southern route if the measure were approved, and he wanted the railroad to run through the Midwest and his home state of Missouri. Benton denounced the bill on two counts — first because the administration had not consulted the House during the negotiation of the treaty, and second because the acquisition of more territory for a transcontinental railroad was unnecessary. He declared that the United States already had available excellent routes long the 34th, 35th, 38th, and 39th parallels. If such a purchase of land was necessary, it could have been made for much, much less land; to back up this last claim, he cited Kit Carson as having said of this region that it was so desolate that "a wolf could not make a living on it."[18] Nevertheless, the House on June 29 passed the necessary appropriation bill by a vote of 103 to 62. The same day President Pierce proclaimed the treaty in effect. The follow-

[17] Quoted in *ibid.*, 139-140.
[18] *Congressional Globe,* 33 Cong., 1 Sess., 1031-1036.

ing day ratifications were exchanged with Ambassador Almonte, and the Mexican minister was handed a check for $7,000,000.[19]

The Gadsden Treaty did bring an end to the tensions between the United States and Mexico — at least, to those tensions on the diplomatic level. However, the purchase left a lingering legacy of Mexican hatred for the "Colossus of the North." And although the money received from the purchase did sustain Antonio López de Santa Anna in office for another year, the hatred it engendered helped hasten his departure from the political scene of Mexico, this time permanently. The dictatorship proved expensive to maintain, and the budget was never balanced. Living on credit, either as an individual or as a nation can never last indefinitely; the bills must be paid at last. When Santa Anna's supply of "silver cannonballs" was exhausted, the generals and the bureaucrats began to turn against the aging dictator. Uniting under the Plan of Ayutla, which called for an end to the Santa Anna government and a new constitution, the Liberals gradually gained strength. Early in August of 1855 the dictator slipped out of Mexico City, and on the 17th he boarded a ship at Vera Cruz and sailed away into exile, comforted by the fact that he had banked a considerable sum abroad for just such a contingency. In the early 1870's he was permitted to return to Mexico City where he died in obscurity and poverty on June 20, 1876.

The United States did gain from the Gadsden Purchase — at long last the country had a route for a southern transcontinental railroad. But the boundary still had to be surveyed.

[19]Malloy, *Treaties,* I, 1107. See also Rippy, *The United States and Mexico,* 148-167; Louis B. Schmidt, "Manifest Opportunity and the Gadsden Purchase," *Arizona and the West,* III (Autumn 1961), 245-264; and Louis B. Schmidt, "Manifest Destiny: The Gadsden Purchase and the Southern Pacific Railroad," Chicago *Westerners Brand Book,* XV (September 1958), 49-56.

Socorro, Texas, where the Hangings Took Place

IX

THE SURVEY COMPLETED

IN THE GULF OF MEXICO off the coast of Texas the night of September 18, 1854, was dark and stormy. A raging hurricane was sweeping the area, sinking many ships and flattening coastal towns. Aboard the steamer *Louisiana* that night, bound for Indianola, was the new United States Boundary Commissioner, Major William H. Emory. The soldier not only was worried about his own safety and that of his party, but also about the instruments that he previously had shipped to the little Texas port; these, he knew, were stacked on a dock awaiting his arrival. The captain of the *Louisiana* kept the vessel pointed into the wind, riding the giant waves that threatened at any moment to swamp his craft. Somehow he kept the ship afloat during the long hours of darkness, and morning brought some slackening of the terrible winds.

When the *Louisiana* arrived at Matagorda Bay on the Texas coast one week later, Emory was greeted by a sight of appalling destruction. The town at Matagorda had been leveled to the ground, and every dock at every settlement around the bay had been leveled to the ground — with one exception. Still standing in the midst of the wreckage was the dock at Indianola on which his instruments had been stored. In addition, Emory found that the storm had improved the channel leading into Matagorda Bay; it had forced the water out to sea at such a rapid rate that the channel had been deepened by two feet.

That the instruments of the Boundary Commission had not been lost during the hurricane was an unusual stroke of good fortune for Major Emory — but he was not a man who depended upon the smile of Lady Luck to accomplish his tasks. Instead, he relied on extensive preparation, based on his knowledge of surveying and of actual conditions in the field, and on his selection of the right personnel. Emory was a sound judge of character; the specialists he selected to collect and compile information about the country along the border later would rise to the forefront of nineteenth-century scientists. The assistants he employed for the actual survey were trained and dedicated workers. Even the soldiers who accompanied his party were among the best in the Army. Careful planning, extensive personal knowledge, and a wise selection of men — not luck — account for Emory's success in surveying the American-Mexican boundary, a task at which others had failed.

At the conclusion of the Gadsden Treaty, only one portion of the boundary remained to be surveyed: the line from the Rio Grande westward to the junction of the Colorado and Gila rivers. The work on the lower part of the Rio Grande had been completed while Gadsden was negotiating. When the Bartlett survey had halted in December of 1852 because funds were not available, Emory had journeyed to Washington and reported to the chief of the Corps of Topographical Engineers. Within days of his return to the capital, however, Congress voted funds for completing the survey of the Rio Grande from Laredo to the Gulf — this task could safely be completed while Gadsden was in Mexico negotiating a settlement of the disputed Bartlett-Conde line. To head this new Commission, President Millard Fillmore on March 16, 1853, appointed General Robert Blair Campbell, and Emory was chosen as Surveyor and chief astronomer. Like Bartlett, Campbell had no real qualifications for the post of Commissioner other than political connections. Born in Marlboro County, South Carolina, about 1790, Campbell had graduated from South Carolina College (now the University of South Carolina) in 1809. Afterward he earned his living as a farmer. His military career began in 1814 when he was appointed a captain of the state militia; his political career began in 1820 when he made an unsuccessful bid for Congress. In 1821 he went to the state senate for two years; then he was appointed to fill a vacancy in the United States House of Representatives. During the Nullification Controversy of 1832-1833, Campbell was the commanding general of the South Carolina militia. The following year he was elected to the 24th Congress. In 1840 he moved to Lowndes County, Alabama, and shortly after his arrival in that state he was elected to the legislature. From 1842 to 1850 he was the United States Consul at Havana, Cuba. Afterward he moved to San Antonio, Texas, where he was living when appointed Boundary Commissioner. His appointment proved a happy one, for he had sufficient administrative experience to delegate authority and to trust those under him who had ability.

Campbell, Emory, and their well-organized party sailed from New Orleans in May of 1853, bound for Brazos Santiago at the mouth of the Rio Grande. When the steamer arrived at the port, the sea was running too high to cross the bar and enter the bay;

Brownsville Texas

— *From Emory,* Report, *Part I, page 60.*

therefore they had to lay off and wait until the sea smoothed out. That evening the captain gave orders for the pilot to point the vessel into the wind under a small head of steam. Then he retired for the night, leaving the mate in charge. Emory did not go to bed for he thought the mate "a silly young man, addicted to intemperance." While dozing on the upper deck, the soldier was awakened by the sound of the breakers; the mate had allowed the vessel to head toward shore. Emory ordered the helmsman to turn the wheel and called for the engineer to put on full steam. The ship missed destruction by the narrowest of margins. The next day Emory used the pilot's boat to go ashore, "thoroughly disgusted with my sojourn aboard the steamer."[1]

This harrowing introduction to the lower Rio Grande Valley did not delay the survey, however. The work proceeded speedily, Emory doing the work and Campbell signing the papers. By September the work had been done, and Emory left for Washing, leaving a few men behind to place the boundary markers. He spent the winter and spring of 1853-1854 at the capital preparing his reports and making his maps. Just as he completed this task, President Franklin Pierce was looking for a Commissioner and Surveyor to run and mark the new boundary established by the Gadsden Treaty. Both tasks were assigned to Major Emory on August 4, 1854.[2]

By the terms of the new agreement, Emory was required to reach El Paso by October 1. Therefore he had to enroll men and gather supplies very rapidly. Then he divided his Commismission into two parts, one to go to El Paso and work its way west under his personal directions, the other to sail to San Diego and push overland to Fort Yuma and begin the survey eastward

[1]Emory, *Report*, I, 53-54.
[2]A copy of this appointment is in *ibid.*, xvi.

under Lieutenant Nathaniel Michler. Born in Pennsylvania, Michler was a graduate of West Point, class of 1848. He had served as Emory's principal assistant during the survey of the Rio Grande in 1851-1852 and again in the Campbell survey of 1853. Emory knew the young officer to be competent and trustworthy. During the Civil War Michler would rise to the rank of brigadier general. He died in 1881.

Under orders from Emory, Michler sailed from New York on September 20, 1854, reaching San Diego by way of Panama and San Franisco. With his four principal assistants and a corps of attendants he reached Fort Yuma on December 9. There he secured a military escort — Company I of the 1st Artillery, commanded by Lieutenant Francis E. Patterson. Early in 1855 the Mexican party arrived to work with him; in charge was Francisco Jiminez, and with him was a military escort under the command of Captain Hilarion Garcia.[3] The Mexican captain is best known in Southwestern history as the last presidial commander at Tucson before the arrival of American troops.

Emory took eleven principal workers and a small party of attendants with him to New Orleans. There he boarded the steamer *Louisiana* bound for Indianola. He reached the Texas port on September 25 after some difficulties with a hurricane. Knowing that he could not reach El Paso by the designated rendezvous of October 1, and also knowing the dangers of rushing ahead personally and leaving the organization and supplying of the Commission to subordinates, he chose to send a runner ahead to El Paso to inform the Mexican Commissioner that he would be delayed. By October 25 Emory had his men and animals ready for travel, along with a military escort of the 7th Infantry commanded by Captain E. Kirby Smith. The captain was another

[3]"Report of Lieutenant Michler," *ibid.*, 101-113.

graduate of West Point, class of 1845. Later he would become a full general in the Confederate Army, commanding all Southern territory west of the Mississippi River. During the Emory survey, he not only commanded the troop escort but also acted as a botanist; the Smithsonian Institution published a report of his observations.

After an uneventful trip by way of San Antonio, Emory arrived at El Paso on December 2. He discovered there that the Mexican Commissioner was none other than José Salazar, with whom he had worked so well previously. Without argument or fuss, the two quickly agreed to the necessary work, which began immediately. Emory discovered that the Mexican government was so anxious to receive the $3,000,000 it was to get upon the completion of the survey that Salazar granted the Americans the right to make its own observations, which the Mexicans would later check. By January 11, 1855, the initial point of 31° 47′ had been ascertained, and the following day the Commissioners agreed to the erection of a rough monument at the spot. This ceremony was conducted on January 31.[4]

Running the line west for one hundred miles, then turning due south to 31° 20′ and finally westward to 111° west longitude proved to be a routine task. The only interruption to the work came when Salazar was imprisoned by his government, which believed (with strong reason) that their Commissioner had too many ties with the deposed Santa Anna. However, Salazar was released within a month, and the survey continued. Little money was forthcoming from Mexico City, and like General Conde before him Salazar was left to his own devices to pay his men. During the course of this survey, Emory had no difficulty with the Apaches—he never trusted them close enough

[4]Journal of the Joint Boundary Commission, *ibid.,* 26-28.

View of the Initial Point on the Rio Grande

— *From Emory,* Report, *Part I, page 60.*

to camp for them to cause any trouble. He later stated about these savages:

> ... I never trusted them; and during the last year of my experience with them I gave orders to permit none to come into any camp under my orders, and to kill them at sight. By taking this harsh but necessary step, I was the only person passing through this country who did not incur difficulty and loss. The Mexican commission was robbed repeatedly, and on more than one occasion was, in consequence, obliged to suspend its operations.[5]

When Emory reached the 111th meridian, he became angry with Lieutenant Michler for the younger officer's failure to meet him at that spot. Michler soon arrived with a suitable explanation of his delay, however, and with a report that the survey had been completed westward. With a Mexican escort under Captain Hilarion García, presidial commander at Tucson, he had surveyed the twenty English miles (twenty-eight miles) of the Colorado River and the line between there and the 111th meridian. On October 15, 1855, the last of the field work was completed. At long last the boundary between the United States and Mexico was surveyed! There remained only the task of drawing and signing the official maps and of preparing and publishing the final report of the survey. Emory suggested — and the American Secretary of the Interior followed the proposal — that the final $3,000,000 due on the purchase not be paid Mexico until the maps were completed and signed. These were exchanged in Washington on June 25, 1856.[6]

[5] *Ibid.*, 88.

[6] Journal of the Joint Boundary Commission, *ibid.*, 35-38. See also William H. Goetzman, *Army Exploration in the American West, 1803-1863* (New Haven: Yale University Press, 1959), 153-208; this excellent study utilizes many manuscript sources and contains a fine short account of the entire boundary survey. Edward S. Wallace, *The Great Reconnaissance* (Boston, 1955), likewise covers the Bartlett and Emory surveys. For the government documents relating to the Emory survey, see *Senate Executive Document* 57, 34 Cong., 1 Sess.

Despite the fact that immediately following the Gadsden Purchase the Territory of New Mexico had extended Doña Ana County westward to include all of the newly acquired area south of the Gila, Captain García and the Mexican detachment at Tucson did not abandon the city until March 10, 1856. New Mexico was very slow to extend its jurisdiction over the area, and never did it actually exercise complete control in the Gadsden Strip. Within two years after the ratification of the purchase, the residents of Gadsdonia (as some called the region) began agitating for separate territorial status, for the American settlers of the region were anxious to have law and order in their communities. American troops did not arrive in Tucson until November 14, 1856, and shortly afterward hoisted the United States flag at the abandoned presidio.[7] The Gadsden Purchase then officially became a part of the United States.

It took Major Emory two years to prepare the full report of the boundary survey under his direction. The first part of this report was printed in 1857; parts two and three had to wait until 1859 because of the necessary work in classifying the scientific data and making the plates. Part one of *Emory's Report of the United States and Mexican Boundary Survey* contains the major's "Personal Narrative," as well as the report of Lieutenant Michler. Emory's narrative is colored with his opinions about interracial marriages (which he thought bad), the Indians of the Southwest (whom he thought savage and barbaric for the most part), and the Mexican population (which he thought degenerate). Also included are comments about the probability of minerals, about the towns along the way, and about the general geography, along with tables of distances and charts show-

[7]Dr. B. Sacks, "The Origins of Fort Buchanan: Myth and Fact," *Arizona and the West,* VII (Autumn 1965), 217.

ing the astronomical and geodetic work. The maps which accompanied the report, and which were printed with it, were the finest ever made to that time. They contained 208 separate points of latitude and longitude from the Gulf of Mexico to San Diego, California. The most prophetic comment contained in the report was Emory's statement that the Rio Grande was constantly shifting in its bed, and that disputes with Mexico were bound to arise.[8]

Appended to part one of the report is the "Geology and Palaeontology" of the boundary region, compiled from the collections and notes of Dr. Charles Christopher Parry, who had accompanied both Bartlett's and Emory's commissions. In addition to this, Parry also wrote the introduction to the section "Botany of the Boundary," which appears in volume two, part one, of the report. In the years following the survey, Parry devoted his summers to field work in the American West; he was the first botanist in the Department of Agriculture, and between 1869 and 1871 worked at the Smithsonian organizing the plant collections. He died in 1890, leaving behind a long bibliography, many close friends, and a far greater knowledge of the Southwest.

Drafting the final report on "Geology and Palaeontology" was the eminent geologist James Hall of Albany, New York. Hall had been born in Massachusetts in 1811, graduated from Rensselaer School in 1832, then began a career that would rank him among the forefront of nineteenth-century geologists. In 1843 he published a report on the fourth geological district of New York which immediately became a classic in that field of

[8]The quarrel over the Chamizal area at El Paso, Texas, just recently settled, is only one of many such disputes. For a study of this question, see Gladys Gregory, "The Chamizal Settlement: A View From El Paso," *Southwestern Studies,* I (Summer 1963).

science. That same year he was commissioned to prepare a report on the paleontology of the state, a project that took him fifty years to complete. At the same time that he was preparing the boundary survey notes for publication, he was serving as state geologist for Iowa and Wisconsin. Later he became director of the New York State Museum and, in 1893, state geologist. He was a strong, forceful man who allowed nothing to stand in his way; thus he was a man with strong friends and bitter enemies. But of his work there can be few criticisms, for his reputation was worldwide and his influence without measure.

Volume two of the Emory report, appearing in 1859, was divided into two parts. The first part dealt with the botany of the boundary and the second with the animals. The general introduction to the part on botany was written by Dr. Charles C. Parry, as stated above. Next came a survey of the general botany, compiled and classified by John Torrey, who at the time was a United States assayer in New York City. Torrey, born in 1796 in New York, received the M.D. degree in 1818 from the College of Physicians and Surgeons, but he was most interested in the plants of the northeastern United States. Soon his reputation became such that most of the plants collected by exploring expeditions in the West were turned over to him for study and report. He also was a professor of chemistry at the United States Military Academy, at the College of Physicians and Surgeons, at Princeton, and at Columbia University, and he served as the state botanist of New York after 1836. When the Assay Office was established in New York City in 1863, he accepted the post for it gave him the opportunity to travel in the West and see many of the plants he had so carefully studied in the laboratory. He died in 1873.

The cacti of the Southwest were so striking that a separate section of volume two, part one, was devoted exclusively to this subject. George Engelmann of St. Louis was the compiler and classifier of that part of the Emory report. Engelmann had been born in Germany in 1809, where he graduated from the University of Wurzburg in 1831 as an M.D. The following year he journeyed to France, then sailed for America. In 1833 he arrived in St. Louis where he began the practice of medicine, as well as the study of local plants. During those first two years in America he made a trip through the Southwest, thus gaining some first-hand knowledge of the area. Gradually his botanical studies absorbed more and more of his time, and many publications in the field flowed from his pen. Associated with him in some of these endeavors in the field was Dr. Charles C. Parry, who doubtless was responsible for Engelmann's selection to compile the section on cacti for the boundary survey report. A happy choice it was, for Engelmann's work has stood the test of time. He died in 1884.

The major portion of volume two, part two, was the work of Spencer Fullerton Baird, at the time an assistant secretary of the Smithsonian Institution. Born in 1823 in Pennsylvania, Baird graduated from Dickinson College. During these early years he developed an avid interest in natural history, especially in ornithology due to a friendship with John James Audibon. In 1843 he received a Master of Arts degree from Dickinson, where three years later he became a member of the faculty. There he expanded his field of interest to cover fish and reptiles. In 1850 he went to the Smithsonian as an assistant secretary, becoming director of the Institution in 1878. In addition, he served as head of the United States Commission of Fish and Fisheries after 1871, a position he held until his death in 1887. His selection to prepare for publication the information about the mammals, birds, and reptiles along the United States-Mexican boundary was logical, and he did his work to the extreme satisfaction of everyone concerned.

The final section of part two, volume two, was concerned with the fish to be found along the border area. This part was compiled by Charles Frederic Girard, a native of Upper Alsace. Born in 1822, Girard studied in Switzerland, where he came under the influence of Louis Agassiz, the famous naturalist. Agassiz brought Girard to the United States with him in 1847, and three years later Girard was employed by Spencer F. Baird at the Smithsonian Institution to work in what would become the United States National Museum in 1857. In the decade immediately preceding the Civil War, Girard published more than 170 learned papers, mostly dealing with fish and reptiles. Most of the reports dealing with Western explorations during this period carry the name Girard in the section on fish, and Emory likewise chose the young man for this task. While working at the Smithsonian, Girard became an American citizen (1854), and he completed work at Georgetown College for his M.D. (1856). The outbreak of the Civil War found Girard in France, and he decided to stay there for his sympathies were Confederate. He lived in Paris, where he practiced medicine and wrote zoological papers, until his death in 1895.

In addition to these scientists who worked on the Emory report, there were the drawings of several artists, principal among whom was Arthur C. V. Schott. He and the other artists, John E. Weiss and A. de Vaudricourt, were listed officially on the payroll as "assistant surveyors," but the plates they turned out to illustrate the report attest to their skill with canvas and brush. Emory's report, taken as a whole, stands as one of the best of the many reports of military and scientific expeditions probing the American West prior to the Civil War. The topographical work has stood the test of more than a century, and the scientific work therein is regarded with awe and respect to this day.

Between 1891 and 1894 the boundary between El Paso and San Diego was resurveyed and new markers, such as this one, were erected.

— From Senate Doc. 247, 55 Cong., 2 Sess., Part I, page 18.

X

EPILOGUE

OF ALL THE characters involved in the seven-year struggle to survey the southern boundary of the United States, John Russell Bartlett has been most associated in the popular mind with the story. In fact, he rarely is mentioned in history books except for his blundering role as Boundary Commissioner. And yet a total assessment of the man and his contributions to the field of American letters produces a vastly different image. When he left Corpus Christi, Texas, in January of 1853, he returned to his home in Providence, Rhode Island, by way of the Mississippi and Ohio rivers to Cincinnati, then by railroad the rest of the way. No doubt his wife and children gave him a warm welcome, for he had been gone for two and one half years. But he was a discredited man with the Democratic administration that took office in March that year, and the two-volume work which he produced telling of his travels in the Southwest, his *Personal Narrative,* was not printed as a government document. Unlike the reports of Gray, Graham, and Emory, which appeared as Senate documents, Bartlett's work was published by D. Appleton and Company, a commercial firm, in 1854. Shortly after his return, and while he was readying his manuscript for the press, he was saddened by the death of his wife. He married again ten years later.

Bartlett's damaging venture into the troubled waters of national politics had not tarnished his reputation in his home state, however. In 1855 he was elected Secretary of the State of Rhode Island, a position to which he annually was reelected until 1872. Twice during this period he visited Europe in an official capacity — in 1867 as a delegate of the Rhode Island Historical Society to the Archaeological Congress held at Antwerp, and in 1873 as one of the United States Commissioners to the International Prison Congress in London. And more books continued to appear bearing his name — *Bibliography of Rhode Island* (1864); *Index to the Acts, Resolves and Reports of Rhode Island, from 1758 to 1862* (12 volumes, 1856-1863); *The Literature of the Rebellion* (1866); and *Memoirs of Rhode Island Officers in the Service of the Country During the Civil War* (1867).

While Secretary of State for Rhode Island, Bartlett entered upon the Herculean task of classifying and arranging all the documents of the secretary's office — some 25,000 manuscript items — which then were bound in 192 volumes, thus making them more readily available for scholars to use. Even all these activities did not fully occupy his time, however, for during the same period he edited and published the ten-volume *Records of the Colony and State of Rhode Island, 1636-1792,* the cost being borne by the state. Each of these volumes was illustrated with documents, letters, and notes, many of which came from the private collection of John Carter Brown, a wealthy book lover and collector of Providence. Bartlett had given generously of his time and knowledge in helping Brown to acquire one of the finest collections in the world of early Americana, and even before he stepped down as Secretary of State for Rhode Island he was busy preparing and seeing through the press a catalog of Brown's holdings. Part one of the catalog, consisting of three hundred titles of works printed before 1600, appeared in 1865. Part two, dealing with books printed between 1600 and 1700 and containing 1,152 titles, was issued the following year. Part three, covering the years 1701 to 1771, appeared in 1870; and part four, for the years 1771 to 1800, was published in 1871.

As the bibliographer of the John Carter Brown Collection, Bartlett rendered a real service to scholars, and he set a high standard in American bookmaking. Because of later additions to the Collection dealing with the very early period of American history, the ex-Commissioner republished part one of the guide in 1875, this time with six hundred titles. And in 1882 part two was reissued and contained 1,642 titles. At the same time that he was doing this work, Bartlett was busy with other books. In 1879 came *Genealogy of the Russell Family,* and in 1880 appeared the *Naval History of Rhode Island.* A "paralysis of the heart" brought Bartlett's long and fruitful career to a halt on May 28, 1886. At the time of his death, he was characterized by one of his friends as a "scholar and a gentleman,"[1] a fair epitaph and a true appraisal.

John Russell Bartlett knew little or nothing about international diplomacy. He was unfamiliar with conditions in the Southwest, and he proved unable to organize and direct the men under his command. Thus he was a failure as Commissioner of the boundary survey. By several trustworthy estimates he

[1]Charles Deane, *Proceedings of the American Antiquarian Society,* IV (October 1885-April 1887), 179-185.

spent approximately half a million dollars in total appropriations during the two and one half years he worked in the Southwest, but only about $100,000 of this sum actually went for running and marking the Guadalupe Hidalgo line. The rest was wasted through mismanagement and on jaunts through the countryside. Yet strangely enough, the misapplied $400,000 was a wise investment for the American taxpayer in the long run. In return the country received the *Personal Narrative.* The publication of this work in 1854 marks a high point in Southwestern literature. The two-volume *Personal Narrative* has been footnoted so many times that its value to scientists and historians is well known; in addition, it was for many years the standard guide for travelers coming to or passing through the area. It was readable, reliable, and factual. Bartlett provided pictures and maps, and he inserted profiles of the leading men of the region. How much easier the historian of the Southwest would find his task if every five years or so the government had sent a Bartlett through to see and to record his findings. Bartlett's failure as Boundary Commissioner was really a failure of the American political system which made it possible for him to secure the appointment. Perhaps the most charitable assessment of the man is still that he was a "scholar and a gentleman."

The man who bore the brunt of the survey, Major William H. Emory, was rewarded for his work by a promotion to brevet lieutenant colonel. And he deserved it, for his work was completed on time and with extreme harmony between himself and the Mexican Commissioner — as contrasted with the delays and quarrels of the Commission headed by John Russell Bartlett. In his introductory remarks to his report, Emory was justified in expressing pride in his accomplishment, as well as in the saving he had effected for the government. He noted that a total of

$787,112 had been appropriated by Congress since 1848 for surveying the boundary according to the Treaty of Guadalupe Hidalgo, and yet that survey had never been completed. On the other hand, he noted that the total cost of the survey as delineated by the Gadsden Treaty was only $103,780, leaving on hand some $135,800 not expended out of the total appropriation.[2]

Once the paper work concerned with his report was completed, Emory rejoined his regiment, the Second Cavalry, which was then serving in Kansas. He arrived in time to participate in some of the border difficulties then in progress in "Bleeding Kansas," and was a member of the Utah expedition of 1858 in connection with the so-called Mormon War. The following year he was transferred to the Indian Territory (Oklahoma), but was given a leave of absence from that assignment in 1860 to serve as a member of the board of officers convened to revise the course of instruction at West Point. At the outbreak of the Civil War, a Confederate official offered Emory the rank of major general with the Southern forces. However, Emory indignantly refused. Instead he gathered the troops under his command and hastened them toward Fort Leavenworth just ahead of a force of four thousand rebels. He arrived at Fort Leavenworth on May 31 without the loss of a single man, horse, or wagon. He thus was the only officer on that frontier to bring an entire command out of the insurrectionary territory. These five companies of cavalry, seven companies of infantry, and four pieces of artillery subsequently aided far beyond their mere numbers in keeping Missouri within the Union camp, for they restored the confidence of prominent local citizens in the government's ability to defend the area.

[2]Emory, *Report,* I, 21-22.

During the winter of 1861-1862 Emory commanded a regiment charged with the defense of Washington. The following spring he participated in the Manassas and Virginia Peninsula campaigns, so distinguishing himself that he advanced to the rank of colonel. Later he saw service in Louisiana, commanding the defenses at New Orleans and fighting in the Red River campaign. In 1865 he was promoted first to brigadier and then major general of volunteers, and was placed in charge of the Department of West Virginia. In 1866 he was mustered out of the volunteer service and made commander of the Department of Washington. Subsequently he headed the District of the Republican, and then in 1871 he returned to Louisiana as commander of the Department of the Gulf. He retired from the army on July 1, 1876, as a brigadier general. Those who knew him well declared that his stern exterior and quick temper covered a warm, sympathetic nature. His wife was Matilda Wilkins Bache, a great granddaughter of Benjamin Franklin. They maintained their permanent home in Washington, D.C., and it was there that Emory died on December 1, 1887.[3] Despite his fine record as a fighting man, won during the Mexican and Civil Wars, Emory is best remembered for his work as a Topographical Engineer. His *Notes of a Military Reconnoissance* was an excellent piece of work, and the *Report on the United States and Mexican Boundary Survey* confirmed his early promise and permanently established his reputation.

Andrew B. Gray, the Surveyor unwittingly caught up in the maelstrom of national politics and fired from the Boundary Commission, was employed in 1853 by the newly organized Texas Western Railroad to survey a thirty-second parallel route

[3]George F. Price, *Across the Continent with the Fifth Cavalry* (New York, 1883), 210-223.

for a transcontinental railroad. This he completed successfully, but the road was never built. During the Civil War Gray served as a captain in the Confederate forces. While examining the Mississippi River between Port Hudson and Fort Pillow, he was killed by the explosion of the boiler of a steamer.[4] Gray was an honest and forthright man, one who saw his duty and tried to do it — for which an ungrateful government fired him.

Lieutenant Amiel Weeks Whipple, shortly after the Bartlett survey ended, was placed in charge of the thirty-fifth parallel railroad survey. This was perhaps the most important possible route for a railroad, for it seemed the most likely compromise in the fight between northerners and southerners over the location of the transcontinental line. Whipple assembled his party at Fort Smith, Arkansas, in July of 1853 and set out westward. His principal assistant on this survey was Lieutenant Joseph Christmas Ives, who would gain prominence in Southwestern history for his attempts to push the head of navigation on the Colorado northward from Fort Yuma. The route of survey led from Fort Smith to Albuquerque and the Zuñi villages, then to the Colorado River, which was crossed near present Needles, and finally terminated at the Pacific shore.[5] Whipple rose rapidly during the Civil War, reaching the rank of major general of volunteers for gallant and meritorious service. He died on May 7, 1863, of wounds received during the Battle of Chancellorsville in Virginia. Fort Whipple, Arizona, was named for him.

[4]For the story of the thirty-second parallel report, as well as for additional biographical details, see L. R. Bailey (ed.), *The A. B. Gray Report* (Los Angeles: Westernlore Press, 1963).

[5]See A. W. Whipple, *Report of Explorations for a Railway Route near the Thirty-Fifth Parallel . . .* , in *Reports of Explorations and Surveys, Senate Executive Document* 78, 33 Cong., 2 Sess. (This is volume 3 of the set usually referred to as *Pacific Railroad Reports*).

The other characters connected with the controversial boundary survey likewise found their destinies, some of them good, others tragic. John B. Weller went on to become governor of California, dying in 1875.[6] The drunken Colonel John McClellan after his recall was placed in charge of the Tennessee River surveys and died in 1854. McClellan's replacement with the Boundary Commission, the quarrelsome Colonel James D. Graham, was assigned to duty on the Great Lakes superintending harbor improvements; he died in 1865 while having charge of the repair of harbor works from Maine to the Chesapeake area. Surveyor, and later Commissioner, José Salazar of Mexico went on to head the commission that surveyed the boundary between his nation and Guatemala. He supported the French adventure that brought Maximilian to the Mexican throne, and died in disgrace and poverty in Mexico City in 1892.

Had the protests of Andrew B. Gray been heeded and the southern boundary of New Mexico been set at 31° 52′ north latitude, in keeping with the intent of the treaty makers of 1848, there would have been little need for the United States to make a large purchase of territory in 1853. Gray's interpretation of the boundary as established by the Treaty of Guadalupe Hidalgo would have secured for the United States the necessary route through the mountains for a southern (*i.e.*, a thirty-second parallel) transcontinental railroad, thus making unnecessary the cession which was the essential feature of the Gadsden Treaty. Had Gray's opinion prevailed, all the land south of the Gila might well have remained under the jurisdiction of the Republic of Mexico — and this indeed would have altered significantly

[6]For an extended biographical sketch of Weller, see H. Brett Melendy and Benjamin F. Gilbert, *The Governors of California* (Georgetown, Calif.: The Talisman Press, 1965), 81-90.

the subsequent history of the American Southwest. In fact, had the United States waited only a few short months until the Whipple survey of the thirty-fifth parallel route was surveyed, it would have realized that the Gadsden Purchase was unnecessary. Whipple's report would have provided sufficient ammunition for those opposing the Gadsden agreement to have prevented its ratification in the United States Senate.

The entire controversial boundary survey, beginning in 1848 and ending in 1853 (there was no controversy on the Gadsden Treaty survey), should serve as a lesson in the folly of political appointment to posts requiring technical and diplomatic skills. The eleven decades that have elapsed since those events have shown, however, that the United States did not profit from the mistakes of that fiasco. It has been said that a politician is a man who wins elections. All too often in the American experience ex-politicians — those who have held office and failed to win reelection — become boundary commissioners or receive other posts where they can blunder about in fields in which they have no knowledge or competence. It has been a national delusion in this country that the holding of elective office educates a man in administrative affairs, thus qualifying him to head anything.

Yet although the controversial boundary survey did not teach any lessons or impart any wisdom to Washington politicos, it did lead to the purchase of an extremely valuable strip of territory, one that has more than paid for itself in subsequent mineral and agricultural production. The one lasting tragedy of this affair is that the United States did not purchase more territory from Mexico while it had the chance. The history of the Southwest since 1853 would have been far different had this nation secured a port at the mouth of the Colorado River. It is expecting too much of politicians with an eye on the next election, however, to believe that they actually had in mind the best interests of a region where there were no constituents for those representatives who had a voice in setting the boundary. The Southwest must, therefore, be grateful for what it did gain in this prolonged comedy of errors.

BIBLIOGRAPHY

For additional biographical information on Boundary Survey personnel, see the *Dictionary of American Biography* or Francis B. Heitman, *Historical Register and Dictionary of the United States Army* (2 vols., Washington, 1903). Government documents used in this study are not included in this bibliography, except for the few which were abbreviated, in the belief that the information in the footnotes is sufficient to find them.

Almada, Francisco R. *Diccionario de Historia, Geografia, y Biografía Sonorenses.* Chihuahua City: Ruiz Sandoval, 1952.

———. "Governadores del Estado: Gral. D. Angel Trias," *Boletín de la Sociedad Chihuahuense de Estudios Historicos,* III (July and August 1941), 172-188.

Almonte, Juan Nepomuceno. *Proyectos de Leyes sobre Colonizacion.* Mexico City: Ignacio Cumplido, 1852.

Arista, Mariano. *Colonias Militares.* Mexico City: I Cumplido, 1848.

Arrowsmith, Rex. *Mines of the Old Southwest.* Santa Fe: Stagecoach Press, 1963.

Bailey, L. R. (ed.). *The A. B. Gray Report.* Los Angeles: Westernlore Press, 1963.

Baldwin, P. M. "A Historical Note on the Boundaries of New Mexico," *New Mexico Historical Review,* V (April 1930), 116-137.

Bartlett, John R. Letter to J. R. Moore (Holliday Collection, Arizona Pioneers' Historical Society, Tucson).

———. *Personal Narrative of Exploration and Incidents . . . .* New York, 1854. Reprinted in 1965 by Rio Grande Press, Chicago.

Bartlett, Richard A. *Great Surveys of the American West.* Norman: University of Oklahoma Press, 1962.

Bolton, Herbert Eugene. *Guide to the Materials for the History of the United States in the Principal Archives of Mexico.* Washington, 1913.

"Boundary Line: Trials and Adventures of the Surveyors as Described by General Frank Wheaton," Tucson *Arizona Daily Citizen,* July 27, 1895

Brandes, Ray. *Frontier Military Posts of Arizona.* Globe, Arizona: Dale Stuart King, 1960.

Brinckerhoff, Sidney B., and Faulk, Odie B. *Lancers for the King*. Phoenix: Arizona Historical Foundation, 1965.

Callcott, Wilfrid Hardy. *Santa Anna: The Story of an Enigma Who Once Was Mexico.* Norman: University of Oklahoma Press, 1936.

Calvin, Ross (ed.). *Lieutenant Emory Reports.* Albuquerque: University of New Mexico Press, 1951.

Carson, William G. B. (ed.). "William Carr Lane, Diary," *New Mexico Historical Review*, XXXIX (October 1964), 274-332.

Conde, Pedro García. *Ensayo estadistica sobre el Estado de Chihuahua.* Chihuahua City: Imprente del Gobierno a Cargo de C. Ramos, 1842.

Cremony, John C. *Life Among the Apaches.* San Francisco: A. Roman & Company, 1868. Reprinted in 1951 by Arizona Silhouettes, Tucson.

Deane, Charles. Obituary to John R. Bartlett in *Proceedings of the American Antiquarian Society,* IV (October 1885-April 1887), 179-185.

Dobyns, Henry F. (ed.). *Hepah, California! The Journal of Cave Johnson Couts.* Tucson: Arizona Pioneers' Historical Society, 1961.

Edwards, E. I. (ed.). *The Whipple Report.* Los Angeles: Westernlore Press, 1961.

Emory, William H. *Report of the United States and Mexican Boundary Commission, Senate Executive Document* 108, 34 Cong., 1 Sess. 2 vols. Reprinted in 1967 by the Rio Grande Press, Chicago.

Faulk, Odie B. "The Controversial Boundary Survey and the Gadsden Purchase," *Arizona and the West*, IV (Autumn 1962), 201-226.

———. "A Letter from John R. Bartlett at Camp Yuma, 1852." *The Journal of Arizona History,* VI (Winter 1965), 204-213.

———. "John Russell Bartlett and the Southwest: An Introduction," in John R. Bartlett, *Personal Narrative* . . . (2 vols., Chicago: Rio Grande Press, 1965).

———. "William H. Emory: Soldier, Engineer, Diplomat," in William H. Emory, *Report* . . . (2 vols., Chicago: Rio Grande Press, 1967).

Forbes, Jack D. *Warriors of the Colorado.* Norman: University of Oklahoma Press, 1965.

Foreman, Grant. (ed.) *A Pathfinder in the Southwest: The Itinerary of Lieutenant A. W. Whipple During his Exploration of a Railway Route from Forth Smith to Los Angeles in the Years 1853 and 1854.* Norman: University of Oklahoma Press, 1941.

Garber, Paul Neff. *The Gadsden Treaty.* Gloucester, Massachusetts: Peter Smith, 1959. Facsimile reprint of the 1923 original.

Goetzman, William H. *Army Exploration in the American West, 1803-1863.* New Haven: Yale University Press, 1959.

———. *Exploration and Empire: The Explorer and Scientist in the Winning of the American West.* New York, 1966.

Gray, Andrew B. "Report of A. B. Gray, with a map in relation to the Mexican boundary," *Senate Executive Document* 55, 33 Cong., 2 Sess.

Gregory, Gladys. "The Chamizal Settlement: A View From El Paso," *Southwestern Studies,* I (Summer 1963).

Hammond, George P. (ed.). *The Treaty of Guadalupe Hidalgo.* Berkeley: Friends of the Bancroft Library, 1949.

Hanighen, Frank C. *Santa Anna: The Napoleon of the West.* New York, 1934.

Horn, Calvin. *New Mexico's Troubled Years.* Albuquerque: Horn and Wallace, 1963.

Kelleher, William A. *Turmoil in New Mexico, 1846-1868.* Santa Fe: The Rydall Press, 1952.

Kelly, Charles. "Antoine Leroux — Pathfinder," *The Desert Magazine,* VIII (October 1945), 5-9.

Ladd, Horatio M. *History of the War With Mexico.* New York, 1883.

Lesley, Lewis B. "The International Boundary Survey from San Diego to the Gila River, 1849-1850," *Quarterly of the California Historical Society,* IX (March 1930), 1-15.

Lockwood, Francis C. *Thumbnail Sketches of Famous Arizona Desert Riders.* Tucson: University of Arizona Press, 1946.

Loyola, Mary. "The American Occupation of New Mexico," *New Mexico Historical Review,* XIV (July 1939), 267-273.

McPherson, William (ed.). *From San Diego to the Colorado in 1849: The Journal and Maps of Cave J. Couts.* Los Angeles: The Zamorano Club, 1932.

Malloy, William M. *Treaties, Conventions, International Acts, Protocols and Agreements Between the United States of America and Other Powers, 1776-1909.* 2 vols. Washington, 1910.

Manning, William R. *Diplomatic Correspondence of the United States: Inter-American Affairs, 1831-1860.* 12 vols. Washington, 1932-1937.

Matthews, William R. "An Answer to a Century-Old Question," Tucson *Arizona Daily Star,* September 15, 1965, F-10.

Melendy, H. Brett, and Gilbert, Benjamin F. *The Governors of California.* Georgetown, California: The Talisman Press, 1965.

Memoria que la direccion de Colonizacion é Industria. Mexico City: G. Torkes, 1851.

Miller, David Hunter (ed.). *Treaties and Other International Acts of the United States of America.* 8 vols. Washington, 1942-1948.

Ochoa, Humberto Escoto. *Integración y Desintegracion de Nuestra Frontera Norte.* Mexico, 1949.

Ogle, Ralph H. "Federal Control of the Western Apaches," *New Mexico Historical Review,* XIV and XV (October January 1940), 30-365 and 12-71.

Paredes, M. *Proyectos de leyes sobre Colonización y Comercio en el Estado de Sonora.* Mexico City: I. Cumplido, 1850.

Parkhill, Forbes. *The Blazed Trail of Antoine Leroux.* Los Angeles: Westernlore Press, 1966.

Price, George F. *Across the Continent with the Fifth Cavalry.* New York, 1883.

Prucha, Francis P. *A Guide to the Military Posts of the United States, 1787-1895.* Madison: State Historical Society of Wisconsin, 1964.

Raht, Carlysle Graham. *The Romance of Davis Mountains and Big Bend Country.* Odessa, Texas: The Rahtsbook Company, 1963.

Reglamento para el Establecimiento de las Colonias Militares en la Frontera del Norte. Mexico City: Imprenta del Govierno, a Cargo de José M. Sandoval, 1869.

Rippy, J. Fred. "A Ray of Light on the Gadsden Purchase," *Southwestern Historical Quarterly,* XXIV (January 1921), 235-242.

———. *The United States and Mexico.* New York, 1921.

Rives, George L. *The United States and Mexico, 1821-1848.* 2 vols. New York, 1913.

Robles, Manuel. *Memoria del Secretario de Estado y del Despacho de Guerra y Marina.* Mexico City: Vicente G. Torres, 1852.

Sacks, Dr. B. "The Origins of Fort Buchanan: Myth and Fact," *Arizona and the West,* VII (Autumn 1965), 207-226.

Salazar, José Ylarregui. *Datos de los trabajos astronomicos y typograficos despuestos en forma de diario. Practicados durante el año 1849 y principio de 1850 por la Comision de limites Mexicana en la linea que divide esta republica de la de los Estados-Unidos* . . . . Mexico: Juan R. Navarro, 1850.

Schmidt, Louis B. "Manifest Destiny: The Gadsden Purchase and the Southern Pacific Railroad," Chicago *Westerners Brand Book,* XV (September 1958), 49-56.

———. "Manifest Opportunity and the Gadsden Purchase," *Arizona and the West,* III (Autumn 1961), 245-264.

Sears, Louis M. "Nicholas P. Trist, Diplomat with Ideals," *Mississippi Valley Historical Review,* XI (June 1924), 85-98.

SED 34. *Senate Executive Document* 34, 31 Cong., 1 Sess., 2 parts.

SED 119. *Senate Executive* 119, 32 Cong., 1 Sess.

Smith, Ralph A. "Indians in American-Mexican Relations Before the War of 1846," *Hispanic American Historical Review,* XLIII (February 1963), 34-64.

Stevens, Robert C. "The Apache Menace in Sonora, 1831-1849," *Arizona and the West,* VI (Autumn 1964), 211-222.

Wallace, Edward S. *The Great Reconnaissance.* Boston, 1955.

Ward, John. "Indian Affairs in New Mexico under the Administration of Willian Carr Lane," ed. by Annie H. Abel, *New Mexico Historical Review,* XVI (April and July 1941), 206-232, 328-358.

Wharton, Clarence R. *El Presidente: A Sketch of the Life of General Santa Anna.* Austin, Texas: Gammel's Book Store, 1926.

Woodward, Arthur. *Feud on the Colorado.* Los Angeles: Westernlore Press, 1955.

———. (ed.). *Journal of Lt. Thomas W. Sweeny, 1849-1853.* Los Angeles: Westernlore Press, 1956.

———. *Lances at San Pascual.* San Francisco: California Historical Society, 1948.

Zorrilla Luis G. *Historia de las Relaciones entre Mexico y Los Estados Unidos de America, 1800-1958.* 2 vols. Mexico City: Editorial Porrua, 1965-1966.

INDEX

BOOKS OF THE WEST . . . FROM THE WEST

3 5132 00238 5565
University of the Pacific Library

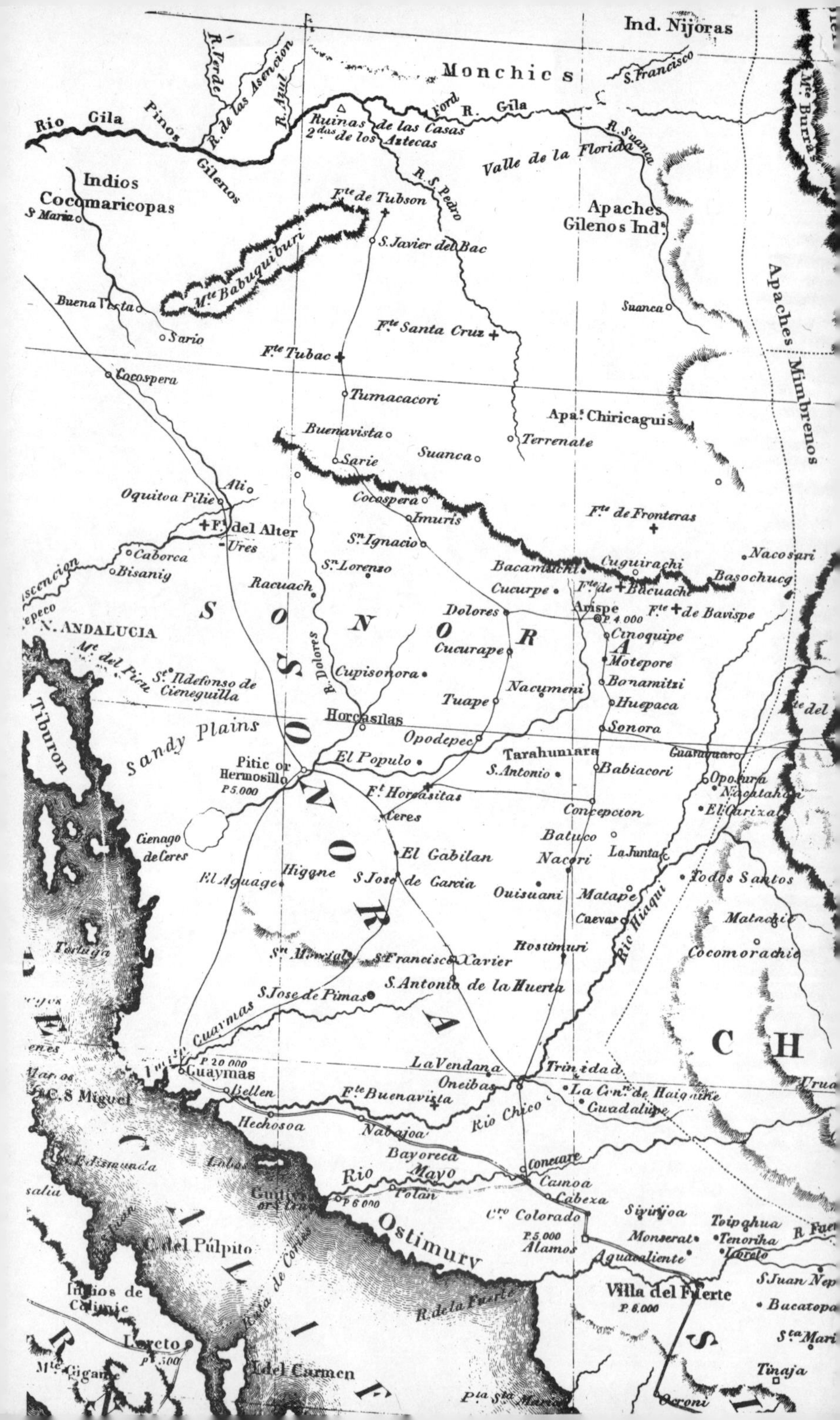
Ind. Nijoras
Monchics
S. Francisco
R. Verde
R. de las Asencion
R. Azul
Rio Gila
Pinos
Gilenos
Ruinas de las Casas
2das de los Aztecas
Ford
R. Gila
R. Suanca
Valle de la Florida
R. S. Pedro
Indios
Cocomaricopas
S. Maria
Fte de Tubson
S. Javier del Bac
Apaches
Gilenos Indˢ
Mte Babuquiburi
Mte Burras
Buena Vista
Sario
Suanca
Apaches
Fte Santa Cruz
Fte Tubac
Cocospera
Mimbrenos
Tumacacori
Apaˢ Chiricaguis
Buenavista
Terrenate
Suanca
Sarie
Ali
Oquitoa Pilie
Cocospera
Imuris
Fte de Fronteras
Fˢ del Alter
Ures
Sn Ignacio
Caborca
Bisanig
Sn Lorenzo
Nacosari
Bacamuchi
Cuguirachi
Basochucg
Cucurpe
Fte de Bacuachi
Racuach
Dolores
Arispe
P. 4.000
Fte de Bavispe
N. ANDALUCIA
SONORA
R. Dolores
Cucurape
Cinoquipe
Motepore
Bonamitzi
Cupisonora
Sn Ildefonso de
Cieneguilla
Nacumeni
Tuape
Huepaca
Tiburon
Horcasilas
Sonora
Sandy Plains
Opodepec
Tarahumara
El Populo
Pitic or
Hermosillo
P. 5.000
S. Antonio
Babiacori
Fte Horcasitas
Ceres
Concepcion
Cienago
de Ceres
Batuco
Nacori
La Junta
El Gabilan
El Aguage
Higgne
S. Jose de Garcia
Quisuani
Matape
Todos Santos
Cuevas
Rio Huiqui
Tortuga
Hostimuri
Cocomorachie
S. Francisco Xavier
S. Antonio de la Huerta
S. Jose de Pimas
Cuaymas
CH
P. 20.000
Guaymas
LaVendana
Trinidad
Oneibas
La Conᶜⁱᵃ de Haiqui
C. S. Miguel
Fte Buenavista
Rio Chico
Guadalupe
Hechosoa
Nabajoa
Bayoreca
Lobos
Conicare
Rio Mayo
Camoa
Cabeza
Polan
P. 6.000
Cro Colorado
Sivirijoa
Ostimury
P. 5.000
Alamos
Monserat
Tenoriha
Aguacaliente
Loreto
C. del Púlpito
Villa del Fuerte
P. 6.000
Ruta de Cortes
R. de la Fuerte
Loreto
Mte Gigante
I. del Carmen
Bacatopa
Tinaja
Pta Sta Maria
Oeroni